Soul After Trauma

A History of the Soul and a New Architecture of Survival, Reintegration and Hope

Albert Baye Schriber

Albert Baye Schriber

Contents

Preface

Why the Soul, Why Now

I did not begin this book as a scholar. I began it as a person who, at the midpoint of what I had taken to be a perfectly coherent life, found that coherence quietly dissolving from the inside. Some of that dissolution belonged to the ordinary shocks by which a life discovers its own limits. Some of it belonged to older wounds and forms of survival whose consequences I had carried longer than I knew. I had a profession, relationships, and habits of thought I trusted. I had, I believed, a reasonably clear sense of who I was. And then, as tends to happen when we are mistaken about ourselves in ways we cannot yet see, the questions arrived not as philosophical propositions to be examined at a comfortable distance, but as experiences demanding something from me personally. What am I, under all of this? What persists when the roles fall away? What in us fragments to survive, and what in us still longs to become whole? What is the soul, and does it still mean anything to ask?

These questions are very old. They are, in fact, among the oldest questions recorded in human writing. The Egyptians were asking them four thousand years before the Common Era. Plato gave them a systematic form that we are still arguing about. The Psalms cried them into the face of an answering sky. Augustine turned them into literature of such searing honesty that they remain, seventeen centuries later, among the most intimate words ever written. And Jung, the figure who became my unexpected companion through the years it took to write this book, spent his long life showing that these questions do not originate in philosophy or theology alone. They arise from the psyche itself, unbidden, in the middle of ordinary lives, in dreams and crises, in breakdowns, survivals, and the sudden, inexplicable sense that the life one has been living is not quite one's own. The history of the soul is therefore not only a history of ideas. It is also a history of how human beings have tried to survive fracture, name their depths, and return, however partially, to wholeness.

I came to Jung, as many people do, through a door that had nothing to do with academic interest. A therapist recommended *Memories, Dreams, Reflections* at a moment when I needed, more than anything, evidence that someone had taken the inner life seriously as a serious thing, not as a symptom, not as a malfunction, but as the primary site of a human being's deepest work. Jung provided that evidence with a candor and intellectual courage I found disarming. He did not pretend that the unconscious was tidy, that the soul was simple, or that transformation was a technique one could apply and complete. He had his own midlife collapse, his own encounter with material he could barely manage, and he documented it with a humility that still matters. He was a scientist who refused to pretend that the soul was small enough to fit inside his methodology. For someone trying to understand not only suffering but survival, not only injury but the possibility of reintegration, that refusal was not a luxury. It was a form of permission.

What took me from that personal encounter to this book was the growing realization that Jung is not, in any simple sense, a new development in the history of the soul's self-understanding. He is, at his best, recovering and rearticulating older wisdom in a language the modern West could hear. Every tradition I have examined in the years of research behind this manuscript was already exploring much of the same territory he charted, often with greater structural sophistication than he is usually given credit for. The Egyptians mapped the soul's multiple layers. Plato described the psyche's inner warfare. The Hebrew prophets understood that the deepest encounter with the divine was also the deepest encounter with oneself. Augustine discovered that the interior has no bottom. Ibn Arabi located an entire ontological realm between the purely spiritual and the grossly material and, with the precision of a cartographer, named it the imaginal world. John of the Cross described, from the inside, the dissolution of everything the ego mistakes for the soul. These were not primitive gropings toward a truth that only the modern period could formulate. They were genuine discoveries, expressed in the idioms available to each tradition, and Jung was among the modern thinkers who recognized how much they still had to teach us.

This book is my attempt to trace that recovery: to follow the soul's self-understanding from its earliest recorded expressions through the ruptures and recoveries of the medieval and modern periods, through Freud's courageous if incomplete descent, through Jung's deeper and still-unfinished excavation, and into the terrain we now inhabit. But it is not only a historical study, and not only a Jungian one. It is also an attempt to describe the soul as a living architecture of survival, fragmentation, reintegration, and hope: a way of understanding how wounded people endure, how the psyche protects what it cannot yet integrate, and how wholeness may become possible again without denying the fracture that made survival necessary. We live in a digital age that is, in certain respects, among the greatest challenges the soul has faced, and in other respects, a moment of urgent return, when older wisdom may help us name the difference between mere functioning and genuine healing.

I write as a wounded survivor who has lived through abuse and carried its consequences, as someone who has read deeply, learned slowly, and earned a Ph.D. in philosophy that became, for me, the tool to think and write with greater clarity about what I had lived. I do not write as a clinician, and I do not claim to have the answers to heal what wounds a person, a family, or a culture. I write as a witness who studied, a philosopher by training, a researcher, and a human being by necessity. I have tried to be fair to every tradition I examine, understanding each on its own terms before reading it through a Jungian lens, and to acknowledge when the Jungian reading illuminates and when it oversimplifies. I have tried to write with the warmth this subject deserves and the rigor it demands. I have tried, most of all, to write the book I needed when the questions first arrived, and the book I suspect others may need when survival is no longer enough, and the deeper question becomes how a wounded life might still be gathered into meaning.

If it reaches you at the right moment, some of it may read like recognition rather than argument, the strange, quiet sense of finding words for something you already, somewhere, knew. That experience, Jung might say, is not a coincidence. It is the soul identifying itself in its own mirror. And for those who have been wounded, fragmented, or forced to survive by living in pieces, that recognition may also be something gentler and more demanding: the first hint that what broke to protect you was not the end of your story, and that the work of becoming whole, however slow, remains possible.

Introduction

Mapping the Territory

The word "soul" has fallen on hard times. In the Western academic tradition, it is often regarded with a mixture of suspicion and embarrassment as a pre-scientific concept that careful thinkers replaced, first with "mind," then with "brain," and most recently with various computational metaphors that reduce the person to a processing system, more or less sophisticated in its pattern-recognition. Outside the academy, the word persists in vernacular use: soul music, soul food, the soulful gaze. But in these usages, it has become almost entirely sentimentalized, stripped of the metaphysical seriousness it carried for three thousand years. We use it when we want to invoke warmth, depth, or authenticity, but we no longer quite mean anything systematic by it, and we are uneasy when pressed to say what we do mean.

This book is a sustained argument that this evacuation of seriousness was a mistake, a costly and consequential mistake with identifiable philosophical roots and identifiable psychological consequences. It is also an attempt at recovery: a tracing of the concept of the soul through the great traditions that took it seriously, an examination of the philosophical and cultural forces that dismantled it, and a reconstruction, drawing primarily on the depth psychology of C. G. Jung, of what a contemporary, post-critical account of the soul might look like. Not a return to pre-critical credulity, but a genuine advance: a soul-concept that has passed through the acids of modern skepticism and emerged with its essential reality still intelligible. What follows is therefore not only a history of the soul. It is also an effort to describe the soul as a living architecture of survival and healing: the structure within which wounded lives fragment, endure, and, under the right conditions, move toward reintegration.

The argument this book makes can be stated, though its development requires length and care. Every major tradition that has grappled seriously with the question of the soul has arrived at a cluster of related insights: that the soul is not a simple, unified substance but a structured multiplicity; that it exists on several simultaneous levels personal, relational, and transpersonal; that it develops through an encounter with its own depths, including its own darkness; that this process is never complete; and that it unfolds in relationship to others, to tradition, and to the numinous dimension of experience that every culture has known by different names. These insights appear in Egypt four millennia ago, in Plato's dialogues, in the Hebrew Psalms, in Augustine's *Confessions*, in Ibn Arabi's breathtaking metaphysics, in John of the Cross's night, and in the clinical consulting rooms of modern depth psychology. They converge, I will argue, because they are descriptions of the same structural reality: the psyche as it is, beneath the personality we construct for daily use. They also help explain why trauma can fracture a life without abolishing its deeper center, and why hope is not sentimentality but the possibility that what has been divided may yet be brought into truthful relation again.

Jung serves as this book's interpretive thread not because he was the first to understand the soul, but because he understood it in a way that can still speak across the boundary between ancient metaphysics and modern clinical experience. He read the ancient traditions Egyptian, Greek, Gnostic, alchemical not as historical curiosities but as primary documents in the history of the psyche's self-understanding. He recognized in his patients' dreams imagery that appeared in myths they had never read, from cultures they had never encountered. He took this not as evidence of cultural diffusion but of a shared psychic substrate, what he called the collective unconscious, that underlies individual experience and connects each living psyche to the accumulated depth of human soul-making. This is a remarkable claim, and I will examine it critically throughout this book. But it is also, as the traditions surveyed here suggest, a claim with very deep roots.

The book is organized into five parts. Part I examines the ancient soul: Egypt, Greece (Plato, then Aristotle), the Hebrew tradition, and the Stoic-Neoplatonic synthesis. Part II examines the medieval soul: Augustine, Aquinas, the great Islamic philosophers (Avicenna and Ibn Arabi), and the Christian mystical tradition culminating in John of the Cross. Part III traces the modern soul's dissolution and attempted recovery: Descartes's fateful bifurcation, the empiricist problematic of personal identity, Nietzsche's anguished individuation without a container, and Freud's courageous but partial descent into the unconscious. Part IV turns to the psychological soul: Jung's full architecture, the ethics of the shadow, trauma and dissociation, and the contemporary clinical validation provided by Internal Family Systems therapy. Part V opens onto the evolving soul: questions of immortality, alchemical transformation, a proposed four-layer model, the psychic challenges of the digital age, the practice of active imagination, the possibility of collective individuation, and, in the final chapter, the soul's vocation as humanity's deepest unfinished project. Taken together, these five parts do more than narrate a history. They also propose an architecture: a way of understanding survival, fragmentation, reintegration, and the forms of hope available to wounded souls without denying the reality of their wounds.

Jung appears in every chapter, not as a corrective bolt-on but as a natural reading, the way one reads any difficult text through the best available interpretive tradition. Sometimes the Jungian reading illuminates dimensions of a tradition that the tradition itself could not name. Sometimes the tradition illuminates dimensions of Jung that his own clinical language obscures. The dialogue is genuine, not staged. The traditions examined here do not need Jung to legitimate them; they are profound in their own right. But their depth often becomes more navigable when held in conversation with the most comprehensive depth psychology the modern West has produced.

One final word about what this book is not. It is not a survey of religious history, nor a comparative mythology, nor a clinical psychology textbook. It is a work of philosophical synthesis, an attempt to think across traditions, to find the structural commonalities beneath their surface differences, and to ask what those commonalities reveal about the soul's actual nature. It is also, unavoidably, a personal book. Philosophy at its best is always personal, not in the sense of being merely autobiographical, but in the sense of being written by a person genuinely invested in the questions. I am genuinely invested in these questions. The soul, I have come to believe, is not an optional topic for those with spiritual interests. It is bound up with the central dramas of human life: how we live, how we relate, how we suffer, how we endure, and how we grow. Getting it wrong, or refusing to ask the question at all, has consequences we are living with. Getting it right, or at least less wrong, may be among the most important intellectual and spiritual tasks of our moment. That is what this book reaches for — not only a more adequate history of the soul, but a more truthful account of how wounded souls survive, and how they may yet become whole enough to hope.

Part 1 - The Ancient Soul

Chapter One
The Egyptian Soul

Participating in the Cosmos

To enter the Egyptian understanding of the soul is to leave behind, at the threshold, almost every assumption Western philosophy has handed us. The soul, in the Egyptian world, was not one thing. It was not a substance, not a faculty, not a ghost inhabiting a machine. It was a constellation multiple, simultaneous, functional, and cosmic, and the Egyptians mapped its components with a precision that has no analog in the Western philosophical tradition until Carl Gustav Jung began, in the early decades of the twentieth century, to discover similar structures in the dreams of his patients. The convergence is not accidental. It is the psyche recognizing itself.

The most familiar of the Egyptian soul-components is the *ka*, often translated as the vital double or the life force. The *ka* was born with the individual and remained as a kind of spiritual twin, not identical to the person but the person's animating principle, the pattern of vitality that distinguished a living being from a corpse. At death, it did not simply vanish; it required sustenance (hence the elaborate provisions in Egyptian tombs), a name by which it could be called, and a body or its representation to inhabit. The *ka* was not merely biological vitality, however. It was transpersonal in character: the pharaoh's *ka* was understood to be the *ka* of all the kings before him, an accumulated royal vitality flowing through the individual like an electric current through a wire. What the Egyptians grasped, without the vocabulary of depth psychology, is that the individual self is animated by something that exceeds it. This life principle is not self-generated but received, inherited, and participated in.

If the *ka* was the vital double, the *ba* was the personality in its most mobile and relational form. Depicted as a human-headed bird, a striking image for what cannot quite be confined, the *ba* moved between the world of the living and the world of the dead, between the individual and the divine, between the tomb and the cosmos. The *ba* could travel, perceive, and report; it was the soul's capacity for movement and for experiencing what lay beyond the enclosed self. Jan Assmann, the great contemporary scholar of Egyptian religion, describes the *ba* as "the social and communicative aspect of the person," the soul not as a private possession but as a relational capacity, the part of us that is constituted by and capable of genuine encounter. This is precisely the aspect of the soul that the pure Cartesian tradition most completely loses: the self as an island of private rational consciousness has no *ba*. It has nowhere to go and nothing to encounter. The Egyptian soul, by contrast, is a soul-in-relation from the beginning.

The *akh* represents a third dimension: the luminous, unified being that the soul could become through the successful navigation of death and transformation. If the *ka* and *ba* were the soul's functional components during life, the *akh* was what they could become together, the integrated, transfigured being that participated fully in the cosmic order. It is important to note that the *akh* was not automatic; it was an achievement. Not every person who died became an *akh*. The achievement required honest self-examination, ethical integrity, and the willingness to face what Egyptian religious texts described with unsparing clarity: the moment at which the heart is weighed against the feather of Ma'at, truth, justice, cosmic order in the great Hall of the Two Truths. This judgment scene, depicted in countless papyri of the *Book of the Dead*, is the earliest extended record in human history of what we might call the shadow confrontation: the moment at which the soul must face, in the presence of divine witnesses, the full truth of what it has been.

Two further components complete the picture. The name was understood not merely as a label but as an ontological constituent of the person. To know someone's true name was to have a kind of access to their being. To destroy a person's name was to perform a kind of murder reaching beyond physical death: it was to erase the soul's claim on existence. This conviction that naming is a form of being, that language participates in reality, sounds strange to modern ears trained by the Cartesian division of word from thing. But it is precisely what the depth-psychological tradition recovers when it insists that naming the complex, speaking the dream, and giving language to the previously unspeakable inner experience are transformative acts. The *ren* anticipates this insight with remarkable economy.

Finally, the *khaibit* the shadow. The Egyptian shadow was not evil, was not the seat of moral failure, was not to be annihilated or transcended. It was the dark companion, the necessary double of the luminous self, without which the full soul could not be constituted. The shadow followed the person, literally as a shadow follows a body in light. What the Egyptians understood, and what Jung spent much of his career recovering, is that the shadow is not the soul's enemy but its completion: the unlived, the unacknowledged, the aspects of ourselves that require the dark to be seen for what they are. A soul without a shadow is a soul without substance, a luminosity that casts nothing because it admits to being nothing. The Egyptian insistence on honoring the shadow as a genuine component of the soul is one of the most psychologically sophisticated gestures in the entire history of the concept.

Jung adopted the concept of participation mystique from the anthropologist Lucien Lévy-Bruhl to describe the pre-individual mode of consciousness in which the self experiences itself as embedded in and continuous with its world, rather than as isolated and observing it from a distance. For Lévy-Bruhl, this was a primitive stage to be surpassed. For Jung, it was the psychological baseline from which individuation must depart and to which, in a more conscious form, it must return. The Egyptian world was organized around participation mystique at every level: the individual participated in the *ka* of the ancestors, the pharaoh participated in the divine, the dead participated in the cosmic order, the soul participated in the very structure of reality through its alignment with Ma'at. Death was not annihilation but transformation — a passage from one mode of cosmic participation to another. The Field of Reeds, the Egyptian paradise, was not a reward for good behavior; it was a continuation of the soul's life in a more luminous mode of the same participation.

What does Jung need from Egypt? More, I think, than he explicitly acknowledged. The Egyptian soul-complex anticipates, with structural precision, the key components of Jung's model of the psyche. The *ba*, moving between worlds, functions as the anima, the soul-image that mediates between the ego and the unconscious depths, drawing the conscious self into the encounter with what lies below and beyond it. The *ka*, as the transpersonal double that animates the individual without being reducible to individual identity, mirrors the Self: the organizing center of the total psyche, which the ego experiences as both intimate and other, as something given rather than achieved. The *khaibit* is the shadow in its most literal form, not a moral category but a structural one, the darkness that accompanies every light, the companion that cannot be outrun. And the judgment scene in the *Book of the Dead*, the heart weighed against the feather, is the earliest recorded attempt to describe what Jung called the shadow confrontation in the individuation process: the moment at which the soul must see itself whole, without the comfortable edits of the persona.

The Egyptian insistence that the soul has multiple simultaneous layers, functional, relational, cosmic, moral, and linguistic, is not primitive animism. It is a structural insight of profound sophistication, one that Western philosophy largely abandoned when it succumbed to the temptation of simplicity, deciding that the soul must be one thing, of one nature, operating by one principle. Egypt did not need Jung to understand the psyche. Jung, one might say with some precision, needed Egypt to understand what he was finding in his patients: a soul that refused to be simple, that came in multiple components, each with its own logic and its own claims, the whole held together not by the ego's sovereign will but by participation in something larger than any of its parts.

The soul is a constellation. Egypt knew this first. Every chapter that follows is, in some sense, the story of that knowledge, its development, its suppression, and its recovery.

Chapter Two
The Greek Soul I

Plato and the Chariot of the Self

When Plato wishes to say something true about the soul, he reaches for a chariot. The charioteer holds the reins, commanding two horses of utterly different temperament: one noble, white, responsive to reason and aspiring upward toward the divine; the other dark, heavy, straining earthward, responsive only to force. The charioteer is the logos, the rational faculty attempting to govern the soul's competing impulses toward higher and lower goods. The allegory appears in the *Phaedrus*, one of Plato's most visionary dialogues, and it has captivated readers ever since, not primarily because it is intellectually elegant. However, it is, but because it is psychologically true. We know that chariot. We have all felt the reins go slack.

Plato's tripartite soul reason (*logistikon*), spirit (*thumoeides*), and appetite (*epithumetikon*) appear most systematically in the *Republic*, where it serves as the psychological analog of the just city, whose three classes (rulers, warriors, producers) correspond to the soul's three functions. The correspondence is deliberate and illuminating: justice, for Plato, is not primarily a social arrangement but a psychic one the condition in which each part of the soul performs its proper function in right relation to the others. The just soul is not the soul in which reason has annihilated appetite or crushed spirit, but the soul in which these three have found their proper hierarchy and proportion. This is a crucial and often misread point. Plato was not an enemy of the passions. He was an enemy of their disordered rule.

The chariot allegory takes this structural insight and gives it motion, narrative, and urgency. The charioteer strains to hold the dark horse in check while the white horse aspiringly follows the immortal souls themselves chariots, driving the great circuit of the heavens, glimpsing, in their ascent, the Forms: Beauty itself, Justice itself, Wisdom itself. These Forms are not abstractions in the logician's sense. They are realities more real than the things that participate in them, the patterns that make intelligible why anything is beautiful or just or wise at all. The soul's highest aspiration is to see them, to return to them, because the soul, Plato argues in the Meno and the Phaedo, already knows them. Learning is not acquisition but recollection (*anamnesis*): the bringing back into consciousness of what the soul knew before it entered into embodied life.

The doctrine of recollection is, philosophically, an account of innate knowledge. But read psychologically, that is, through the Jungian lens that this book employs, it is an account of the collective unconscious. When Plato's Meno's slave boy, with no formal education, is led through a geometrical proof and arrives at correct conclusions he has never been taught, Plato takes this as evidence that the soul carries knowledge from before birth. Jung, encountering the same phenomenon in a different register, the spontaneous appearance in his patients' dreams of mythological imagery from traditions they had never studied, reached an analogous conclusion. There is inherited psychic content that precedes and exceeds personal experience. The terminology differs; the structural claim is remarkably similar. Both Plato and Jung argue that the psyche is not a blank slate that accumulates knowledge solely through experience. It comes pre-loaded, one might say, with patterns Plato calls them Forms; Jung calls them archetypes that shape experience from within.

The *Symposium* adds another dimension crucial to any soul-history: the figure of Eros as the mediating daemon. Diotima, the wise woman whom Socrates quotes as his teacher, corrects the assumption that Eros is a god. He is a daemon neither fully divine nor fully mortal, and his function is precisely mediation: he carries human offerings to the gods and divine gifts to humans, filling the interval between the two realms and making communication between them possible. Without the daimons, she says, there would be no intercourse between the human and the divine. Eros, specifically, mediates through longing the soul's restless reaching toward what it does not yet have but dimly remembers, the desire for completion that no earthly object can permanently satisfy. It is this Eros that Diotima traces, in her celebrated ladder of ascent, from the love of a single beautiful body upward through the love of all beautiful bodies, then of beautiful practices, then of beautiful knowledge, until finally the initiate beholds Beauty itself the Form that all earthly beauties participate in.

Jung's transcendent function occupies the same structural position as Plato's Eros-daemon. The transcendent function is not a faculty but an event: it arises when the tension between conscious and unconscious contents becomes sufficiently acute, and produces a third thing a symbol that neither side of the opposition could have generated alone. The symbol is the "third thing" that carries the psyche forward, mediating between what the ego knows and what the depths are pressing for. This is exactly what Eros does in the *Symposium*: he is the mediating symbol that arises in the tension between the human and the divine, the known and the unknown, the ego's current position and the Self's pull toward wholeness.

But it is the chariot that most squarely earns its place in the psychological canon, because it is honest about what the rational tradition tends to elide: the dark horse does not disappear. The charioteer's skill is not defined by the permanent defeat of the lower horse but by the ongoing, effortful, never-finally-resolved governance of both. Plato understood what the entire classical tradition of virtue ethics understood and what the modern rationalist tradition forgot: the psyche is not naturally unified, not naturally rational, not naturally inclined toward the good. It must be cultivated, governed, managed through education, through practice, through the long labor of habituation. And even the most excellently governed soul still has two horses, not one.

Jung puts it with characteristic directness: the shadow cannot be annihilated, only integrated. The dark horse in Plato's chariot is not the enemy to be slain. It is the energy to be redirected the chthonic vitality that, when not acknowledged, pulls the chariot off the road, but when properly acknowledged and governed, provides the very power that drives it. The charioteer who denies having a dark horse loses control of the chariot. The charioteer, who is nothing but a dark horse, runs the chariot off the cliff. Wisdom is the middle way that requires both horses to function and knows which is which.

Plato's Forms, finally, function in his system precisely as archetypes function in Jung's: not as the objects of detached intellectual contemplation but as the organizing principles of experience itself. We do not first encounter many beautiful things and then abstract the concept of Beauty. We encounter beautiful things as beautiful because Beauty as an archetype a pre-existing pattern shapes our perception from within. The Forms are not conclusions; they are preconditions. The chariot allegory, the doctrine of recollection, the Eros-daemon, the tripartite soul all of these converge on a single, psychologically resonant insight: the soul is at war with itself, it knows more than it consciously possesses, it is driven by a love it cannot entirely understand, and its highest task is not the elimination of its complexity but the increasingly wise navigation of it.

Plato did not solve the problem of the dark horse. He did something more valuable: he named it honestly, mapped its power accurately, and insisted that wisdom consists not in transcending the contest but in governing it well. Two thousand four hundred years later, Jung said the same thing in a different language. Neither of them was wrong, and neither of them was finished.

Chapter Three
The Greek Soul II

Aristotle and the Soul as Form

Aristotle is, in many respects, the greatest corrective in the history of philosophy. Where Plato reached toward transcendence, Aristotle remained steadfastly on the ground. Whereas Plato's soul was essentially at war with the body it inhabited, imprisoned in matter and longing for the pure realm of Forms, Aristotle's soul was the body's own organizing principle. This form made the body the kind of body it was. The soul, he famously wrote in the *De Anima*, is the first actuality of a natural body that has the potential for life. It is not a separate substance that could, in principle, exist without the body; it is what makes the body a body of this kind rather than a heap of elements. If the eye were an animal, sight would be its soul. The soul is the capacity; the body is the capacity's substrate.

This is a radical departure from Plato, and its consequences run throughout the Western philosophical tradition. By locating the soul in the living activity of the organism rather than in a transcendent realm from which it is imprisoned, Aristotle makes the soul empirically accessible in a way Plato's could never be. We do not find the soul by turning away from the body and ascending through reason to the Forms. We find it by attending carefully to what living things do, how they grow, how they perceive, how they move, how they think. The soul is not hidden behind experience; it is disclosed by it.

Aristotle's hierarchy of souls nutritive (shared by all living things, responsible for growth and reproduction), sensitive (shared by animals and humans, responsible for perception and desire), and rational (distinctively human, responsible for thought) is not a ranking of metaphysical substances but a ranking of capacities. Higher capacities presuppose and include lower ones: the sensitive soul presupposes the nutritive, the rational presupposes the sensitive. Human beings are not pure rational intellects who happen to have bodies; they are organisms whose rational capacity is built upon, and continuous with, their animal and even vegetative nature. We think based on what we sense; we sense based on what we live. The soul is layered, and the layers are not separable in life, whatever they may be in philosophical analysis.

The concept of *hexis*, a formed disposition, a habituated state of character, is among Aristotle's most psychologically fertile ideas. A *hexis* is not an isolated act or impulse; it is a settled orientation, formed through the repetition of particular kinds of acts until those acts become, as we say, second nature. Courage is not a single brave act; it is the *hexis* of acting bravely in the appropriate circumstances, formed by the many times one has acted bravely before. The courageous person does not debate with themselves in the moment of crisis; they act from the depth of a character formed by accumulated experience. The soul, in Aristotle's account, is not what you are in principle; it is what you have become through the choices you have made and the habits they have laid down.

Jung's concept of the complex is the depth-psychological equivalent of the Aristotelian *hexis*. However, it reaches into dimensions that Aristotle did not explore and lacked the clinical tools to observe. A complex, in Jung's technical sense, is an autonomous psychic constellation, a cluster of feeling-toned images and memories organized around a central archetype that behaves with a consistency and urgency that transcend the ego's conscious intentions. Like a *hexis*, the complex is not chosen in the moment of its activation; it is the deposit of a history, usually an emotionally charged history of repeated experience. The mother complex, for instance, is not the mere memory of one's actual mother but the entire psychic constellation built up around the archetype of the mother: the accumulated impressions, the fears, the longings, the projections, all organized into a psychic structure that operates autonomously, activating in predictable ways when the appropriate triggers appear. The complex, like the *hexis*, is what the soul has become through what has repeatedly happened to it.

The crucial difference, and it is not a small one, is that Aristotle's *hexis* is primarily conscious and voluntary in its formation; it is the product of choices made, however habitual they become, while Jung's complex is formed largely outside conscious awareness, often as the product of experiences the person did not choose and could not control. This difference reflects the depth-psychological revolution's central insight: much of what shapes the soul is neither chosen nor conscious, nor transparent to rational inspection. Aristotle's soul is formed by deliberate practice; Jung's is formed by everything that happens to us, including what happens below the threshold of awareness. Both are right. Together, they describe the full range of soul-formation.

Aristotle's most tantalizing and most contested claim concerns the active intellect, the *nous poiêtikos*. Unlike the passive or potential intellect, which receives forms from sensory experience and is mixed with the body, the active intellect is what illuminates those forms, makes them intelligible, and is, in Aristotle's startling formulation, separable from the body, unmixed, impassible, and by nature immortal. This is a remarkable concession from the philosopher who most consistently insisted on the unity of the soul and body. The active intellect, apparently, is not fully accounted for by the organism's activities. Something in the act of thought transcends the organism that is thinking.

This is the point at which Aristotle's philosophy opens onto the same territory that Jung explored under the name of the Self: the dimension of the psyche that transcends the personal ego, that participates in something universal, that cannot be entirely explained by the individual's biographical history or organic constitution. The active intellect, like the Jungian Self, is the part of the psyche that seems to come from beyond the personal, that illuminates rather than receives, that organizes the rest from a position not fully immanent within it. Aristotle was too cautious or too committed to his empiricism to develop this insight very far. But it is there, luminous in its incompleteness, pointing toward a territory that depth psychology would eventually chart.

Aristotle's most enduring contribution to the history of the soul may be, paradoxically, his most democratic one. By locating soul in the organizing capacity of living organisms rather than in a special spiritual substance available only to rational beings, he made every living thing a bearer of soul in some form. The plant, the worm, the horse, the human being, all are ensouled, each according to its capacity, each possessing the soul appropriate to what it is. The distinctive mark of the human soul is not that it has a soul where others do not, but that its soul's organizing capacity can become conscious of itself. It can know its own knowing, examine its own structure, and reflect on its own nature. This is what Aristotle calls the activity of the rational soul at its highest: *theoria*, contemplative self-knowledge, the soul knowing itself as what it is.

Jung's individuation reaches toward the same point from a different direction: the soul, at the depth of the individuation process, becomes increasingly conscious of its own structure, aware of its complexes, its archetypes, its shadow, its Self, without thereby completing the process, because the process has no completion, only increasing depth and clarity. What Aristotle called *theoria* and what Jung called psychological consciousness are both names for the soul's capacity, its most distinctively human capacity to see itself from within. The soul that cannot do this is not less real, but it is less fully what it can become. And the becoming, as every tradition examined in this book agrees, is the point.

Chapter Four
The Hebrew Soul

Covenant and the Relational Self

The Hebrew Bible lacks a philosophy of the soul in the systematic Greek sense. What it has is something richer and, for our purposes, more revealing: a literature of the soul's experience, its cries, its exultations, its desperate negotiations with the divine, its laments when the divine seems absent, its wonder when the world suddenly opens and the holy blazes through. The Psalms are perhaps the most psychologically honest body of literature ever written, and they repay reading as much as a psychological as a religious document. They are the soul speaking without a filter, in all its contradiction and urgency, and they are addressed; this is the crucial point not to itself but to an Other. The Hebrew soul knows itself only in relationship.

The central Hebrew word for the soul is *nephesh*. It is often translated as "soul," but the translation is misleading if it imports the Greek assumption of a distinct, separable spiritual substance. The *nephesh* is better rendered as the whole living person in their vitality — the breathing, desiring, suffering, rejoicing, mortal being. When the Psalmist cries "My soul thirsts for God, for the living God" (Ps. 42:2), the thirst is not metaphorical. Its longings constitute the nephesh; it is, in its very structure, a creature of desire and orientation. The Hebrew anthropologist Johannes Pedersen observed that the *nephesh* is, more fundamentally than anything else, the locus of desire: it is what wants, what fears, what loves, what suffers. To have a *nephesh* is to be oriented toward the world with one's whole being.

Alongside the *nephesh*, the Hebrew scriptures speak of the *ruach* —

breath, wind, spirit — as the animating dimension of the person. The *ruach* is relational: it is the divine breath breathed into the first human at creation (Gen. 2:7), the wind of God moving over the waters (Gen. 1:2), the spirit that comes upon the prophets and enables them to speak. The *ruach* is not a private possession; it comes from outside and returns to its source. The Hebrew person does not generate their own vitality; they receive it from a source that exceeds them and to which they remain constitutively related. This is the theological formulation of what Jung described psychologically: the ego does not generate its own energy. It receives energy from the Self, the transpersonal organizing center of the total psyche, and the ego that cuts itself off from that source eventually runs dry. The Hebrew insistence on the *ruach* as divine gift rather than personal possession is not a theological decoration but a structural truth about the soul's relationship to what is larger than itself.

The *neshamah,* the most intimate, rarified breath, is the most interior of these dimensions, the point at which the divine inbreathing touches the human being most nearly. Hans Walter Wolff, in his classic study of Hebrew anthropology, describes the *neshamah* as the person's direct participation in the divine life, not a capacity they possess, but a relationship in which they are held. The three-fold Hebrew soul (*nephesh*, *ruach*, *neshamah*) is not a tripartite division of the self into competing faculties; it is a description of the self as constituted at multiple levels of its relationship to the source of its being. The self is not what it is by itself. It is what it is in relation, at every depth.

The covenantal structure of Hebrew religion is the institutional form of this relational ontology. The covenant (berith) is not a contract between independent parties who happen to find a mutual arrangement advantageous. It is a bond of mutual address and response that constitutes both parties in a way they were not constituted before. When YHWH addresses Abraham, Moses, or the prophets, the address is not merely informational; it is formative. It makes something of the person addressed that they were not before. And the person's response, obedience, argument, lament, or praise is equally formative, not of God but of the relationship itself. The covenant is the structure within which the Hebrew soul exists. Outside the covenant, there is no Hebrew soul; there is only an unaddressed, unanswering human animal.

The psychological parallel Jung would draw is to the ego-Self axis: the relationship between the ego, the center of conscious personality, and the Self, the center of the total psyche, personal and transpersonal. Like YHWH addressing the patriarchs, the Self does not wait for the ego's invitation. It addresses the ego through dreams, compulsions, symptoms, and the numinous experiences that break into ordinary consciousness and demand a response. And, as with the covenant relationship, the ego-Self relationship is not a power relationship in which one party dominates and the other submits. It is a relationship of mutual recognition, in which the ego's task is to hear what the Self is communicating and to respond with genuine engagement, which may include, as the Hebrew tradition never shied from showing, argument, protest, and lament.

The lament psalms are, from a depth-psychological perspective, among the most significant soul documents in any tradition. Three moves characterize them: address to God (often in extreme urgency, "How long, O Lord? Will you forget me forever?" [Ps. 13:1]); description of the crisis in the most concrete and unsparing terms; and a turn not always to consolation, but to renewed trust and often renewed praise, sometimes within the same breath as the complaint. What the lament psalms refuse is silence and pretense. They refuse to tell God or themselves that everything is fine when it is not. They refuse to perform a piety that paper over the shadow. And this refusal is not a failure of faith; it is its fullest expression. The God of the Hebrew scriptures is addressed most intimately from the places of most acute suffering, and the person who prays from those places, who does not exile the shadow from prayer, is exercising what Jung would recognize as the most demanding form of psychological honesty.

The Hebrew tradition preserves something that the Greek philosophical tradition, for all its genius, was in constant danger of losing: the soul is not achieved through contemplation alone. It is lived in the body, in history, in community, in the daily navigation of relationships with both the human and the divine. The Greek philosopher could, in principle, achieve the soul's highest state alone, through the disciplined exercise of reason. The Hebrew person could not: the covenant is corporate, the community is essential, the Sabbath belongs to all, the stranger must be welcomed. Individuation, which Jung understood late but understood clearly, is not a solitary achievement. It requires the other, the relationship, the encounter, the beloved, and the community to actualize what would otherwise remain merely potential.

This is the Hebrew soul's deepest gift to the history of the concept: the recognition that the self is never merely its own. We are constituted by the relationships in which we participate, the words that have been spoken to us and by us, the communities that shape us and that we in turn shape. The soul that withdraws from relationship to achieve a pure inner state has not fulfilled itself; it has amputated something essential. The covenant is not a limitation on the soul's freedom; it is the structure within which the soul's freedom becomes real. And the address that comes from beyond the ego, whether we call it YHWH, or the Self, or the numinous, is not an intrusion but the condition of our becoming.

Chapter Five
The Stoic and Neoplatonic Soul

Logos, Pneuma, and the Return

Two of antiquity's most influential philosophical systems, Stoicism and Neoplatonism, shared, despite their many differences, a conviction that became one of the most fertile and most contested ideas in the history of the soul: that the individual psyche is embedded in a structured cosmos that is itself rational, itself animate, itself in some sense alive. The soul does not inhabit a neutral or indifferent universe. It moves through a world that is organized by the same principle that organizes it — a principle the Stoics called *logos*, and which Plotinus, the supreme Neoplatonic philosopher, located in the emanative descent of the One into the many. For both schools, the task of the philosophical life was not to escape the cosmos but to understand one's place within it — and in doing so, to discover something essential about the soul itself.

Stoic physics is, in a phrase that will surprise those who know Stoicism primarily through its ethics, a form of panpsychism. The universe is pervaded by *pneuma* — a tensile, fiery breath that runs through all things and constitutes their rational structure. The *pneuma* is not merely a physical medium; it is the universe's principle of coherence and rationality, the ground of the order that makes scientific understanding possible. In the individual human being, the *pneuma* is the soul, the hegemonikon, the ruling principle whose proper function is to live in accordance with the universal *logos* that structures reality. The good life, for the Stoics, is the life lived in rational alignment with nature: not nature in the Rousseauian sense of prelapsarian simplicity, but nature in the sense of the rational structure of things as they actually are. The sage who achieves this alignment is, in a sense, thinking with the universe's own thought.

The ethical weight of Stoic psychology falls on the distinction between what is "up to us" (*eph' hēmin*) and what is not. Our bodies, our reputations, our social positions, even our health, none of these is truly ours in the sense that matters. What is truly ours is our judgment, our response to events, our capacity to align our wills with what reason recognizes as the logos's own order. The Stoic sage is not invulnerable to suffering; they suffer. But they suffer as free beings because their inner citadel, the rational soul in its proper alignment, is not touched by what happens to them externally. This distinction, which Epictetus, among others, formulated with memorable directness, is both psychologically astute and psychologically partial: it recognizes the ego's capacity for relative independence from circumstances, but it radically underestimates the autonomy of unconscious psychic contents, which Stoic psychology, committed to rational self-governance, had no framework for acknowledging.

Plotinus occupies a different position in the history of the soul, one of the most extraordinary positions in all of philosophy. Writing in the third century CE, he presents a vision of reality as a hierarchical emanation from the One, an absolute, ineffable source beyond being and thought, downward through Intelligence (*Nous*), Soul (*Psyche*), and finally into Matter. The soul is not created by the One; it emanates from it as light emanates from the sun, remaining connected to its source even as it extends into what is most remote from it. This means that the individual soul, your soul, my soul, is simultaneously an individual soul, a participant in the World Soul, and a dim reflection of Intelligence, which itself is a reflection of the One. The soul exists on multiple levels at once, never fully separated from the divine source from which it flows.

This multi-level structure of the soul is, of all the ancient models, the one that maps most directly onto Jung's understanding of the psyche as simultaneously personal, cultural, and transpersonal. The personal level corresponds roughly to Plotinus's individual soul in its embodied, biographical particularity. The cultural and archetypal levels correspond to the World Soul — the shared psychic substrate from which individual souls draw their imagery and deepest patterns. And the One beyond all categories, beyond all thought, corresponds to what Jung called, with appropriate reticence, the Self in its most transpersonal dimension: the ground of the psyche that cannot be described without immediately falsifying it, that can only be pointed toward through symbol and experienced through the numinous encounter. Plotinus's *henosis,* the mystical union with the One that is the soul's highest achievement, is, in Jungian terms, the ego's fullest surrender to and identification with the Self: not the ego's annihilation, but its discovery of the deeper ground in which it has always participated.

The Neoplatonic concept of *epistrophe* return, or the soul's turning back toward its source, is the metaphysical grammar of individuation. The soul emanates outward from the One into the multiplicity of embodied experience, and in doing so necessarily fragments, disperses, and forgets its origin. The philosophical life, the contemplative life, the ethical life is the process of return: a gradual reversal of the forgetting, a reintegration of the dispersed soul into its own depth, until the deepest depth opens onto the source itself. This is not a rejection of the world but a discovery, through the world, of what underlies it. The Neoplatonist does not leave the body to reach the One; they find, in the right kind of engagement with experience, the thread that leads inward and upward.

The tradition of *theurgical ritual action, understood as genuine soul-movement and* embodied participation in the divine, brings the Neoplatonic soul back into the body in a way that pure contemplation might seem to leave behind. Iamblichus, arguing against Porphyry, insisted that contemplation alone is not sufficient for the soul's ascent. The gods must be invoked through concrete, embodied ritual; the soul must act, not merely think, its way toward the divine. Theurgy is not magic in the dismissive sense; it is the recognition that the soul is embedded in matter and cannot transcend matter by ignoring it. Transformation requires the body. It requires action, image, symbol, the concrete enactment of what contemplation has understood.

Jung recognized in this conviction the ancient precedent for his most characteristic therapeutic discovery: that psychological transformation happens not through insight alone but through symbolic action, active imagination, the embodied engagement with the images that arise from the unconscious. The person who merely understands their complexity intellectually has not transformed it. The transformation requires an encounter imaginal, emotional, and embodied with the autonomous psychic content. The Stoic sage commands their soul through rational judgment; the Neoplatonist contemplates the soul's return through hierarchies of being; the theurgist enacts the transformation through ritual that engages body and soul together. Jung's clinical method draws from all three, in different proportions, and finds in each a partial truth that the others complement.

What the Stoics and Neoplatonists share, and what makes their synthesis a crucial moment in the history of the soul, is their shared conviction that the cosmos is meaningful that what happens to the soul is not random, that suffering and transformation are real and intelligible events within a rational order, not noise in an indifferent mechanism. This is not naive optimism. The Stoics were under no illusions about the hardships of embodied life; many of the greatest Stoic philosophers, Epictetus and Marcus Aurelius, wrote from positions of political vulnerability or personal suffering. But they wrote from within a framework that made suffering navigable precisely because it was not absurd. The soul endures because the cosmos is coherent. The logos holds. And the soul that aligns itself with that logos participates, in its own small way, in something imperishable. This is not an easy conclusion to defend in a post-Cartesian world. But it is also, as we shall see, a conclusion to which the deepest movements of the Western philosophical tradition keep returning dressed in different languages, but pointing in the same direction.

Part 2 - The Medieval Soul

Chapter Six
Augustine

Memory, Confession, and the Restless Soul

There is a moment in the first book of Augustine's *Confessions* that has no real precedent in the philosophical literature that preceded it. The bishop of Hippo is addressing God, describing his own infancy, an infancy he cannot remember but can reason about from the behavior of infants he has observed, and he writes: "Thou awakest us to delight in Thy praise; for Thou madest us for Thyself, and our heart is restless, until it repose in Thee." The sentence is extraordinarily compressed. In it, Augustine identifies the soul's defining characteristic: not reason, not sensation, not will, but restlessness, a constitutive longing that is before all conscious desire and that nothing finite will satisfy. And he identifies the structure of the soul's journey: awakening, inquiry, recognition, rest. He wrote it in prayer, addressing God directly, making the *Confessions* simultaneously an autobiography, a philosophy, and a liturgy, a genre unprecedented in the history of Western letters.

The *Confessions* is, among other things, the first extended phenomenology of the personal unconscious. When Augustine describes his years before conversion, the seductions of the theater, the theft of the pears (undertaken not for need but for the sheer pleasure of transgression), the relationships he clung to, and the philosophies he tried on and discarded, he is not merely cataloging moral failures. He is mapping the psyche's interior as a space of competing motivations, some conscious and some not, some virtuous and some contradictory, none entirely under rational control. The brilliant, restless young man who prayed "make me chaste and continent, but not yet" is describing, with clinical precision, what

Jung would call the divided complex: two centers of motivation, each with genuine psychic weight, pulling in opposite directions, neither able to overcome the other through sheer will. Augustine did not lack resolve. He lacked integration. And that is a different problem, one that will not yield to more willpower.

The philosophical linchpin of Augustine's psychology is his account of memory in Book Ten of the *Confessions*. Memory is, he writes, "a vast court," so vast that Augustine himself is astonished by it: "Great is this force of memory, excessive great, O my God; a large and boundless chamber!" In this court dwell not only personal recollections but also the forms of knowledge, mathematical truths, aesthetic intuitions, and logical principles that the mind knew before it remembers having learned them. And more remarkable still is the presence of God. God is not found by looking outward at the cosmos; God is found by going inward, into the vast court of memory, and discovering that the inmost chamber opens onto something that transcends the self. "I entered," Augustine writes, "and beheld with the eye of my soul the Light Unchangeable." The interior, pursued far enough, opens onto what exceeds the personal.

This is the structure of Jungian depth in its most precise formulation: go deep enough into the personal through the persona, through the personal unconscious, through the complexes and their contents and you break through into the transpersonal. The collective unconscious is not the personal unconscious expanded; it is a qualitatively different level of depth, encountered only by those who have gone far enough into themselves to reach the place where the personal self gives way to something it did not generate. Augustine describes this as the discovery of God within. Jung describes it as the encounter with the Self in its archetypal dimension. The languages are incompatible in their metaphysical commitments; their structural descriptions are identical.

This is the structure of Jungian depth in its most precise formulation: go deep enough into the personal, through the persona, the personal unconscious, and the complexes and their contents, and you break through into the transpersonal. The collective unconscious is not the personal unconscious expanded; it is a qualitatively different level of depth, encountered only by those who have gone far enough into themselves to reach the place where the personal self gives way to something it did not generate. Augustine describes this as the discovery of God within. Jung describes it as the encounter with the Self in its archetypal dimension. The languages are incompatible in their metaphysical commitments; their structural descriptions are identical.

Jung would immediately recognize that this is not merely a religious insight. The person in analysis who keeps returning to destructive relationships, who cannot sustain the changes they consciously intend, and who finds themselves, again and again, pulled toward the same patterns they have resolved to leave, lacks neither willpower nor intellectual insight. They are experiencing the pull of a deeply embedded complex, a love in Augustine's sense, that draws the soul in a particular direction with a force that rational resolution alone cannot counter. The individuation process addresses this not by suppressing the pull but by understanding it, by discovering what the complex is actually seeking, what legitimate need it expresses in distorted form, and what the soul truly needs that the complex's chosen objects cannot provide.

The *Confessions* ends not with Augustine's achievement but with his orientation. He does not claim to have arrived; he claims to have been turned. The restlessness has not disappeared; it has been redirected. And this is psychologically exact: the successful individuation process does not produce a person who is no longer restless, no longer drawn by deeper longings, no longer unsatisfied by the finite. It produces a person who knows the direction in which the longing points and can move, however falteringly, in that direction. The restlessness is the engine, not the dysfunction. Augustine understood this before psychology existed to name it, and he expressed it in prose of such transparent honesty that it has never been surpassed as a record of the soul's experience of its own depths.

Chapter Seven
Aquinas

The Soul as Substantial Form

Thomas Aquinas was twenty-one years old when Frederick II, the Holy Roman Emperor, called Aristotle "that great philosopher who outshines all others as the moon outshines the stars." The young Dominican was not alive yet to hear this. Still, by the time he began writing his great syntheses, he had reached a similar conclusion and proceeded, with the systematic patience that was his intellectual signature, to demonstrate that Aristotle's philosophy and Christian revelation were not in fundamental conflict but could be integrated into a coherent account of reality more comprehensive and more honest than either tradition had achieved alone. The result is the most ambitious philosophical-theological synthesis in Western history, and its account of the soul is among its most carefully wrought achievements.

Aquinas follows Aristotle in defining the soul as the substantial form of the body, the principle that makes the body this organized, living, human body rather than a collection of chemical compounds. The soul is not a separate entity that inhabits the body as a pilot inhabits a ship, the Platonic image Aquinas explicitly rejects. It is the body's own intelligibility, its organizing principle, the formal cause without which the body would not be the kind of thing it is. Against the Augustinian tradition's tendency toward a more dualistic view, in which the soul is a kind of spiritual substance that uses the body, Aquinas insists on their genuine unity. The human being is not a soul with a body or a body with a soul. The human being is the ensouled body, or the embodied soul, taken as a single substance.

This commitment to the soul-body unity has practical and moral consequences that Aquinas drew with characteristic care. If the soul and body are genuinely unified, then the soul's proper operations are performed through the body, not despite it. Sensation, emotion, imagination all of these are genuine soul-activities, not mere bodily disturbances that a properly spiritual person would rise above. The emotions (the passions, in Aquinas's terminology) are not the soul's enemies; they are essential instruments of the moral life, requiring not suppression but education the ordered direction toward appropriate objects by the virtues that correct reason habituation forms. Courage properly ordered; temperance properly modulated; prudence properly applied. The intellectual virtues and the moral virtues together constitute the excellent soul, the soul that knows truly and desires well.

Aquinas's argument for the soul's immortality is notably different from Plato's. He does not argue that the soul is immortal because it is simple, self-moving, or participates in the Form of Life. He argues that the soul is immortal because its characteristic operation, the understanding of universals, is not tied to any particular bodily organ. The eye can see only the visible; the ear can hear only the audible. But the intellect can know the universal, the abstract, and the necessary, and what knows the universal is not itself limited to the particular. The particular's dissolution cannot destroy a faculty that transcends the particular. There is something in human intelligence that, in Aquinas's account, already participates in something beyond the mortal organism that houses it.

Jung, reading this with his depth-psychological sensibility, would find it simultaneously illuminating and, in one crucial respect, radically incomplete. Illuminating because Aquinas preserves the soul's genuine orientation toward truth and goodness as structural features not mere cultural preferences but reflections of what the soul actually is and what it actually needs. The natural desire of the intellect for truth (and the natural desire of the will for goodness) are, in Aquinas's account, the soul's built-in compass ,the orientation toward its proper end that is given with its nature. Jung's individuation has a similar built-in teleology: the Self draws the psyche toward wholeness as surely as, for Aquinas, the intellect is drawn toward truth. The direction is intrinsic to the structure.

The incompleteness, however, is significant. Aquinas's account of the soul is an account of its highest functions ,intellect and will ,operating in their proper order toward their proper ends. It is, deliberately and by design, an account of the soul as it should be. What it has no framework for, and what it therefore leaves philosophically unaccounted for, is the soul as it actually is in its full complexity: the irrational, the autonomous, the dissociated, the complex-ridden, the shadow-haunted. The shadow the khaibit, the dark horse, the divided will, has no legitimate place in Aquinas's elegant architecture. It appears, in his moral theology, as sin and concupiscence: the disordering of the soul's proper functions through the weakness introduced by original sin. But this theological framing, while not wrong on its own terms, has the unfortunate consequence of treating the soul's darkness as purely negative as dysfunction to be overcome rather than as psychic content to be understood and integrated.

This is the price of Aquinas's architectonic achievement. His synthesis is marvelously orderly, marvelously comprehensive, and marvelously convincing on its own terms. But its terms exclude from the cathedral all the psychic material that does not fit the rational-volitional model of the soul: the autonomous dream, the obsessive complex, the irrational love that defies rational analysis, the shadow that refuses the education that virtue is supposed to provide. It takes nothing away from Aquinas's genius to observe that what his system most needs and cannot supply is a psychology of the unconscious, a framework for taking seriously the psychic material that reason does not generate and cannot fully command. That framework would require another six centuries to develop, and it would be built not by a Dominican philosopher but by a Swiss psychiatrist who had been reading, among other things, the Dominicans.

Chapter Eight
Avicenna and Ibn Arabi

The Floating Man and the Imaginal World

The Islamic philosophical tradition of the ninth through twelfth centuries preserved, extended, and, in certain respects, surpassed the Greek philosophical heritage it had received through Syriac and Arabic translations of Aristotle and the Neoplatonists. Scholars who know it primarily through its influence on the Latin scholastic tradition, where it enters, filtered through translation, as "Avicenna" and "Averroes," have typically encountered only a portion of its richness. For our purposes, the most significant figures are Ibn Sina, known in the West as Avicenna, and Muhyiddin Ibn Arabi, two thinkers of the highest order who, between them, provide the most precise pre-Jungian mapping of the deep structure of the psyche that any tradition has produced.

Avicenna's "Floating Man" argument, which appears in several of his psychological works, is a thought experiment of remarkable sophistication. Imagine, he says, that a person is created in midair, in complete isolation unable to see, hear, touch, smell, or taste, with limbs extended to prevent any bodily self-awareness through touch. Would such a person be aware of their own existence? Avicenna's answer is yes. They would be immediately, pre-reflexively aware of themselves as a thinking, experiencing subject, even without any input from the senses or awareness of the body's boundaries. This residual self-awareness this irreducible sense of oneself as a locus of experience cannot be derived from the senses, because the senses are eliminated in the thought experiment. It must be something before, and more fundamental than, sensory experience.

Philosophical interpreters have long noted the resemblance to

Descartes's cogito, and it is real. But Avicenna's argument differs from Descartes's in a crucial respect: Descartes is establishing the certainty of the thinking subject as the foundation for a new epistemology. Avicenna describes the immediate self-presence of the soul as an experiential fact a given of awareness rather than a conclusion of an argument. The Floating Man is not a deduction; it is a description. And what it describes is the soul's fundamental character: a center of awareness that is constituted not by its bodily or sensory relations but by its own self-presence. This is closer to the Jungian Self than to the Cartesian cogito: the Self, for Jung, is not the ego's rational self-reflection but the organizing center of the total psyche, which the ego can encounter but not derive from its own deliberations.

If Avicenna provides the philosophical coordinate, Ibn Arabi the twelfth-century Andalusian mystic and metaphysician whose works are among the most extraordinary in any language provides the ontological map. The *alam al-mithal*, the imaginal world or the world of image-forms (translated into Latin scholarship as the *mundus imaginalis* by the French philosopher Henry Corbin, who spent his career making Ibn Arabi accessible to Western readers), is the ontological realm that exists between the purely spiritual and the purely material. It is the world of the autonomous image not the subjective fantasy of individual imagination. Still, a genuine mode of being that has its own geography, its own inhabitants, its own laws, and that is accessible to the soul through visionary experience, dream, and mystical contemplation.

The importance of this concept can hardly be overstated for the history of the soul's self-understanding. Western philosophy, from Descartes onward, has operated with a sharp binary: either something is objective and material (available to the senses, measurable, intersubjective) or it is subjective and mental (private, non-material, available only to the individual who has it). This binary leaves the psyche's most significant content dreams, visions, symbols, images that arise autonomously and carry a charge that is neither purely subjective nor purely objective philosophically homeless. Ibn Arabi's *alam al-mithal* is precisely the ontological space in which this content lives. It is neither purely "out there" nor purely "in here." It is the intermediate realm, the third thing, in which the divine and the human, the universal and the particular, the spiritual and the material genuinely interpenetrate.

Jung's collective unconscious, in its upper register, the realm of autonomous psychic contents that are not merely personal but appear to have an objective character, arising spontaneously with a force and a precision that the ego did not generate and cannot fully explain occupies the same ontological position as Ibn Arabi's *alam al-mithal*. Henry Corbin himself made this connection explicit, and his correspondence with Jung in the 1940s and 1950s was one of the most philosophically significant exchanges of the mid-twentieth century. Both men recognized that what Jung was encountering clinically and what Ibn Arabi had mapped metaphysically were descriptions of the same territory from different directions: the realm of the autonomous image, ontologically real, psychically accessible, irreducible to either pure spirit or pure matter.

Ibn Arabi's concept of *tajalli*, the self-disclosure of the divine through the forms of the world adds a further dimension. For Ibn Arabi, the cosmos is the mirror in which the divine Absolute, the *al-Haqq*, beholds itself by clothing itself in the infinite forms of creation. Each created being is simultaneously itself and a particular self-disclosure of the divine. The mystic's journey is not to escape the world of forms and reach the formless Absolute; it is to see, in and through the forms, their divine ground, to perceive the *tajalli* in the concrete. This is not pantheism; Ibn Arabi was careful to insist on the distinction between the Absolute and its self-disclosures. It is something more subtle: a recognition that the sacred is not absent from the world but disclosed by it, if one has the eyes to see.

This vision maps onto what Jung called the numinous encounter, the experience of the sacred as genuinely other, genuinely powerful, genuinely transformative, encountered not in a realm beyond experience but in the depths of experience itself. The autonomous image that arises in a dream and carries an unmistakable charge of import; the synchronistic event that seems too precisely meaningful to be mere coincidence; the encounter with a person who carries, for a period, a projection of enormous psychic weight these are all, in the Jungian framework, forms of *tajalli*, moments at which the transpersonal self-discloses through the particular. The Islamic philosophical tradition, dismissed in most Western histories of psychology as at best a repository of Greek texts, was in fact producing some of the most sophisticated soul cartography in human history. It deserves, and this book attempts to begin the recovery, its place in the full history of the psyche's self-understanding.

Chapter Nine
The Dark Knight

John of the Cross and the Soul's Descent

John of the Cross is one of the most demanding writers in the tradition of the soul's self-understanding, and one of the most rewarding. A Carmelite friar and poet of the first rank, imprisoned and tortured by his own religious order in the dungeons of Toledo in 1577, he wrote poetry of such concentrated beauty that it survives as literature regardless of its theological commitments, and a prose commentary on that poetry that constitutes the most precise phenomenological account of what he called the Dark Night of the Soul. The Dark Night is not, as popular usage has diluted it, a period of difficulty or depression. It is a specific spiritual process, a structured dissolution of the ego's most cherished spiritual achievements that John describes with the precision of a physician and the honesty of someone who has been through it.

The process unfolds in two stages, each more severe than the last. The first is the Night of the Senses: the withdrawal of spiritual consolations that had previously made prayer, practice, and religious observance pleasurable and rewarding. The person who had found nourishment in the Eucharist, in meditation, in reading, in worship, now finds these practices arid, empty, unrewarding. The sensory and emotional satisfactions of the religious life dissolve. This is not a punishment; it is a purification. The attachments to spiritual consolation the person's investment in feeling the presence of God, feeling progress in virtue, feeling the emotional rewards of a religious life well-lived are precisely the attachments that must be loosened before the soul can receive what the Night is preparing it for.

The second stage, the Night of the Spirit, is incomparably more severe. Here it is not merely the sensory satisfactions of the religious life that dissolve, but the deepest spiritual certainties: the sense of God's presence, the confidence in one's own spiritual progress, the very structures of meaning that organized the soul's life. The person in the Night of the Spirit does not merely feel that prayer is dry or that Mass is unrewarding. They feel, at the most foundational level, abandoned, as though the God they have oriented their entire life toward is no longer there, or never was, or does not care. The theological virtues, faith, hope, charity, are undergoing a purification so radical that they feel, from within, like their opposites: doubt, despair, coldness.

John insists, with a calmness that is itself extraordinary, that this is not pathology. It is not depression, not failure of faith, not spiritual regression. It is the soul's deepest purification the condition under which God can work in the soul at a depth that the ego's prior certainties were actually preventing. The ego's spiritual achievements its consolations, its sense of progress, its virtuous self-image were, unknown to it, acting as barriers to the deeper union that is the Night's goal. The Night is God's surgery. The anesthesia is the very darkness the soul experiences. And the surgery's result the union John describes in the *Spiritual Canticle* and the *Living Flame of Love* is not the ego's triumph but its transformation: a union in which the soul participates in the divine life not through its own achievement but through the relinquishment of everything it mistook for achievement.

Jung's reading of alchemy as a projection of the individuation process provides the most comprehensive psychological parallel to John's Dark Night. The alchemical *nigredo* the first and most frightening stage of the alchemical work, in which the prima materia is dissolved, blackened, and reduced to its most elementary state is the outer projection of the inner process John describes. The blackening is necessary: without it, the gold that the work aims to produce remains imprisoned in its gross form. The dissolution that appears to be destruction is the precondition for the transformation that appears to be creation. The ego that experiences the *nigredo* whether in the alchemical vessel or in the Night of the Spirit experiences it as catastrophic loss. The Self, which initiates it, knows it as necessary surgery.

This reframing suffering as surgery rather than as punishment or pathology is perhaps the most important contribution the Dark Night tradition makes to contemporary psychology. Secular psychology, understandably committed to the relief of suffering, has difficulty maintaining a framework in which some suffering is not merely meaningless pain to be eliminated but a genuinely transformative process to be undergone. The tradition of John of the Cross does not romanticize suffering; John is clear that the Night is terrible and that no one would choose it voluntarily. But it does maintain, from within the experience, that the darkness is structured that it has a direction, a purpose, and an end that is not accessible from within the Night itself but that retrospective understanding can recognize.

There is no bypass. This is perhaps the most uncomfortable thing the Dark Night tradition has to say to a culture organized around maximizing comfort and minimizing discomfort. John insists, with the authority of personal experience and careful theological argument, that the soul cannot be circumvented around the Night and into the union. The Night must be endured. The techniques and John explicitly reject the idea that any technique can accelerate or safely redirect the Night are beside the point. What is required is not competence but surrender: the willingness to remain in the darkness without grasping at any available light, to continue showing up at the prayer that gives nothing, to maintain the orientation without demanding its reward. This is not passive resignation; it is an extraordinarily active form of faithfulness, the more demanding because it is invisible to the spiritual accounting system the ego had previously relied on. The soul that emerges from the Night, in John's account, has been changed at a level that no amount of voluntary spiritual practice could have reached. The soul has been remade. And the agent of the remaking was not the ego, however willing, but the darkness itself or what moves through the darkness.

Part Three - The Modern Soul

Chapter Ten
Descartes

The Cogito and the Exile of the Soul

The sentence that inaugurates modernity is also the sentence that exiles the soul. "I think, therefore I am": *cogito ergo sum*. René Descartes, sitting by a fire in the winter of 1619–1620, or rather in the philosophical thought-experiment the *Meditations* presents, has stripped away everything that cannot withstand systematic doubt: the senses (which deceive), the external world (which might be a dream), even mathematics (which a malicious demon might cause him to misperceive). What remains, undeniable and bedrock, is the thinking itself. Even if he is being deceived, the deceiving requires a thinker who is being deceived. The thinking proves the thinker. The thinker is the soul. And the soul, in this founding moment of Western modernity, is identified entirely and exclusively with conscious rational thought.

The consequences of this identification unfold through the subsequent three centuries of Western intellectual history with a kind of tragic inevitability. By defining the soul, *res cogitans*, the thinking thing, as pure rational consciousness, essentially distinct from the body, *res extensa*, the extended thing, the mechanism, Descartes achieved what he aimed for: a foundation for certain knowledge immune to skeptical assault. He found it. But the price was catastrophic for the history of the soul, because what he expelled from the definition of the soul was precisely what makes the soul interesting, complex, and, in the most serious sense, real.

The unconscious, within the Cartesian framework, is literally impossible. The soul is, by definition, entirely conscious; the cogito is, by definition, fully transparent to itself. If there are psychic contents below the threshold of conscious awareness, and there are, as every clinical psychologist since has confirmed then they are not, strictly speaking, psychic at all in the Cartesian sense. They must be either brain events (neurological processes in the extended substance) or they must be dismissed as philosophically incoherent. Descartes's framework offers no third option. Dreams are not soul-expressions but the brain's random nocturnal activity. Emotions are not the soul's responses to the world but mechanical perturbations in the body's hydraulic system. The dark horse of Plato's chariot has been turned into a machine. And the machine, obviously, does not need to be known; it needs to be managed.

Jung spent his career not refuting Descartes, which is a philosopher's task, but living with the consequences of the Cartesian settlement and responding to the psychic suffering they produced. The patients who arrived in his consulting room were not suffering from external misfortune. They were suffering from the internal consequences of a cultural framework that had systematically denied the existence, the importance, and the claims of everything in the psyche that was not rationally transparent. Dreams were meaningless; they were told their dreams were noise. Emotions were irrational; they were told their emotions were obstacles to clear thinking. The body's wisdom, the intuition's insight, and the image's authority had all been, in the Cartesian cultural framework, demoted to the status of mechanical processes to be overridden by the sovereign rational will. The soul, in any sense recognizable by the traditions examined in the preceding chapters, had been exiled.

The exile had a further, specifically modern consequence that Jung identified with particular precision: the projection of what is excluded from the interior onto the exterior. When the shadow, the dark, the irrational, the repressed, cannot be located inside the psyche (because the psyche, in the Cartesian framework, is by definition rational and transparent), it must be located outside it. The result is the characteristic modern structure of projection: the certainty that the darkness, the irrationality, the danger are located not in oneself but in the other, the other class, the other race, the other nation, the other religion. Cartesian philosophy does not cause racism, nationalism, or religious persecution. Still, the psychological framework it installs the identification of the self with its most rational and light-filled aspects, the systematic denial of its own darkness, makes the culture organized around it peculiarly vulnerable to mass projection dynamics. The Cartesian settlement is not politically innocent.

What Descartes achieved, philosophically, was genuinely remarkable: the discovery of a point of absolute certainty in the middle of radical skepticism. The cogito is a genuine insight. Thinking occurs; something is thinking; that something cannot coherently doubt its own existence. This much stands. But the cogito as a foundation for a complete account of the soul, the identification of the soul with nothing but rational consciousness is precisely the kind of magnificent philosophical error that produces, over centuries, the kind of cultural suffering it produces. The cogito is modernity's founding insight and modernity's original wound. Both things are true, and both must be taken into account if the account is to be honest.

Chapter Eleven

Locke, Hume, and the Problem of Personal Identity

When the Self Comes Apart

The Cartesian settlement held for roughly two generations before its internal tensions produced a new crisis. Descartes had established the soul as rational consciousness and had left the problem of its relation to the body in the awkward hands of the pineal gland. The empiricist philosophers who followed him, Locke, Berkeley, Hume in England and Scotland, largely accepted Descartes's identification of the mind with its conscious contents, but they applied to those contents the rigorous scrutiny of empirical analysis, asking not what reason could establish in the abstract but what experience could actually confirm. What they found was not the stable, unified, transparent soul that the Cartesian tradition assumed. What they found was considerably more interesting and considerably more troubling.

John Locke's account of personal identity, elaborated in the famous chapter of the *Essay Concerning Human Understanding*, grounds the self not in a substantial soul (which Locke is skeptical about) nor in the continued identity of the body (which changes continuously) but in the chain of consciousness specifically, in memory. I am the same person I was at fifteen because I can remember being fifteen; my fifteen-year-old self is the same person as the ten-year-old by the same chain, and so on back through the remembered past. The continuity of conscious memory constitutes Personal identity. This is a genuinely original and psychologically resonant proposal. The self, for Locke, is a narrative continuity the story one can tell about oneself using memory as the connecting thread.

The Jungian reading of Locke's self is immediate: this is the persona as a philosophical category. The persona, the social mask, the consciously maintained identity is precisely the self that memory constructs and narrates. It is the identity that a person has for themselves and presents to others: the coherent story, the remembered roles, the maintained continuity. And like the persona, Locke's memory-self is both necessary and insufficient. It is necessary because without some principle of narrative continuity, there is no stable identity at all, no way to distinguish a person from the random sequence of their momentary states. But it is insufficient because it accounts only for what the person consciously remembers and can narrate which, as every depth psychologist knows, is a small and carefully edited portion of what has actually shaped them. The wound that shaped one's fundamental patterns may not be consciously remembered at all. The complex that organizes one's most important relationships was not chosen and cannot be recounted. The self is much more and much less orderly than the story memory tells about it.

David Hume went further, and in a direction that reveals both the honesty and the limitation of the empiricist method applied to the soul. When he looked inward, with the rigorous scrutiny of a thinker committed to following experience wherever it leads, he could not find a self. He found, in his celebrated formulation, "a bundle or collection of different perceptions, which succeed each other with inconceivable rapidity, and are in perpetual flux and movement." There is no "I" that has the perceptions; there are only the perceptions themselves, in ceaseless succession. The self is not a substance but a construction, a fiction, even, that the imagination imposes on the bundle to generate the sense of continuity that actually no single perception possesses.

Hume's bundle theory is psychologically honest about the ego in a way that most of the tradition preceding it was not. The ego, the center of conscious personality is indeed constructed, contingent, and discontinuous at the level Hume was examining. The empirical ego is not a fixed substance; it is a pattern maintained in the stream of experience by the continuity of habit, memory, and narrative. This much is true, and Jung would agree. But from this accurate observation about the ego's character, Hume drew the conclusion that there is no self at all which is where the clinical evidence points in the opposite direction. Go deeper than the bundle of conscious perceptions which is to say, go into the unconscious, and one encounters not nothing but something that has a remarkable coherence and authority: the autonomous complex, the archetype, and, at the deepest level, the Self as the organizing center of the total psyche. The Self is not the bundle; it is what organizes the bundle. Hume's method, excellent as an account of the ego, failed him as an account of the total psyche because it lacked the tools to probe beyond consciousness.

The late nineteenth-century researchers of the Society for Psychical Research, Frederic Myers, William James, Edmund Gurney, and their colleagues represent the empirical tradition's attempt to go deeper, and to do so with something like scientific method. Confronted by phenomena that empiricist philosophy had no framework for automatic writing, cases of multiple personality, the apparently veridical aspects of certain mediumistic communications they developed the concept of the subliminal self: a dimension of personality that operated below the threshold of normal consciousness, and that appeared, in certain states, to have access to knowledge and capacities that the conscious self-lacked. Myers's great posthumous work, *Human Personality and Its Survival of Bodily Death* (1903), is the fullest expression of this project and, in retrospect, a proto-depth psychology: the first systematic attempt to take the unconscious dimensions of the person seriously as an empirical phenomenon rather than a philosophical embarrassment.

Jung read Myers and acknowledged the debt. What the SPR investigators were actually mapping through the uncomfortable empirical fact of phenomena that didn't fit the Lockean or Humean frameworks was the same territory Jung would chart through clinical analysis and the study of mythology: the transpersonal dimension of the psyche, the layer of psychic content that exceeds the biographical person and connects the individual soul to the accumulated depth of the species. They lacked Jung's synthetic framework; they were working in an empirical tradition suspicious of theoretical overreach. But the phenomena they encountered were real, and their willingness to take those phenomena seriously rather than explain them away in the Cartesian manner makes them genuine, if imperfect, precursors to the depth-psychological tradition this book traces.

Chapter Twelve
Nietzsche

The Übermensch and Individuation Without Shadow

Friedrich Nietzsche came closer to the truth of the soul than any philosopher between Plotinus and Jung, and he arrived at a philosophical disaster. This is not a paradox easily resolved; it is the essential fact of his intellectual biography, and understanding why it happened is one of the most illuminating exercises in the depth psychology of philosophical thought. Nietzsche had the genius to see that the metaphysical frameworks that had previously grounded the soul's meaning, Plato's Forms, the Christian God, and the Kantian moral order, had been fatally undermined by modernity's critical intelligence, and that this collapse required not a new metaphysical framework but a new kind of human being: one capable of creating meaning from within rather than receiving it from without. What he lacked was an adequate account of the shadow, the darkness within the new human being, and that lack cost him everything.

The "death of God" proclamation in *The Gay Science* is not the cheerful atheist's self-congratulation it is sometimes read as. It is an announcement of catastrophe, the recognition that the framework within which Western values had made sense had collapsed, and that nothing adequate had yet been built to replace it. The nihilism Nietzsche feared was not an intellectual position but a psychic event: the experience of a world that has lost its organizing center, in which every value is equally arbitrary, and in which the question "why?" has no answer that does not eventually dissolve in acid. The will to power, Nietzsche's proposed response to this crisis, is not domination but creative self-overcoming: the soul's capacity to generate meaning, to give itself goals, and to affirm its own existence through the exercise of its highest capacities.

Zarathustra is Nietzsche's great thought-experiment in this direction, and, read psychologically, it is also something more intimate and more disturbing. The figure of Zarathustra, the prophet descending from his mountain to teach humanity its own greatness, is not simply a philosophical character. He is, in depth-psychological terms, a figure arising from the unconscious, the kind of autonomous inner figure that Jung would encounter directly in the active imaginations he recorded in what became the Red Book. The speeches of Zarathustra have the quality of received text, of material that came from somewhere other than the author's rational deliberation, shaped by an urgency and a strangeness that exceed the programmatic content. Nietzsche, in writing Zarathustra, was engaged in something very close to active imagination, the breakthrough of the unconscious into conscious form. He did not have a framework that could hold it safely.

The Übermensch is the concept that crystallizes both Nietzsche's deepest insight and his fatal error. As an aspiration, the idea that human beings are capable of more than the herd mentality, the comfortable mediocrity, and the resentment-driven morality of those who cannot affirm their own existence, the Übermensch is a genuine call to individuation. "Man is something to be overcome," Zarathustra says, and this is precisely what Jung means by the individuation process: the movement beyond the ego's current configuration toward a more inclusive and more genuine identity. But the Übermensch lacks a shadow. He has overcome the herd's resentment, but he has not integrated it; he has transcended slave morality, but he has not understood the legitimate needs it expressed in distorted form. He casts no shadow, which means, psychologically, that his shadow is enormous and completely unconscious.

The Eternal Recurrence, the thought experiment of imagining that one must live one's life exactly as it has been, infinite times is Nietzsche's test of the soul's authenticity: can you affirm your life so fully, in every detail, that you would be willing to live it again and again, forever? It is a magnificent challenge and, in Nietzsche's philosophy, functions as the highest possible affirmation of existence. But read through the lens of depth psychology, it is also the shadow's revenge. The person who has denied their shadow, who has identified entirely with their highest aspirations and expelled their darkness eventually meets the darkness in the only way that remains as compulsion, repetition, the eternal recurrence of the very thing they most sought to escape. Nietzsche's breakdown in Turin in 1889 his sudden, permanent madness is, whatever its neurological etiology, symbolically the breaking through of the shadow that the Übermensch's philosophical architecture had no room to contain.

Jung read Nietzsche with the closest possible attention and drew from him two of the most important lessons in his entire intellectual formation. The first is that the God-image in the psyche does not disappear when the metaphysical God is declared dead. It goes underground, becomes unconscious, and returns, inflated because unconscious, as the ego's identification with the divine. The Übermensch is a God-image wearing the costume of secular philosophy. The second is that the most important question is not how to become great but how to remain honest. The person who undertakes individuation without shadow work does not achieve the Self; they achieve an inflated ego mistaken for the Self. Nietzsche's tragedy is the clearest illustration in modern intellectual history of what happens when the soul reaches for depth without developing the honesty to see its own darkness. He reached for gold and found, in the philosophical gold he produced, the very darkness he had not acknowledged.

Chapter Thirteen
Freud

Mapping the Basement

Sigmund Freud did something that neither the philosophers who preceded him nor the neurologists who were his contemporaries had quite managed to do: he took the unconscious seriously as a clinical fact. Not as a philosophical speculation, not as a metaphysical postulate, not as a theological mystery, but as a demonstrable, consequential dimension of the human psyche that could be approached through careful attention to the patient's speech, associations, dreams, and symptomatic behavior, and that, when appropriately understood, revealed a structure susceptible to interpretation and, at least partially, to therapeutic intervention. The courage this required to insist, in the face of a medical culture organized around the neural substrate of behavior, that what a hysterical patient's paralysis meant was as important as its organic mechanism was considerable. Freud had that courage, and he deployed it consistently across forty years of clinical work and theoretical development.

The unconscious Freud discovered was not a gentle or comfortable place. It was the repository of what could not be tolerated in consciousness: the wishes that violated the incest taboo, the aggressive impulses that civilized life required to be repressed, and the infantile longings that adult dignity forbade. The famous iceberg metaphor, the tip of conscious awareness resting on the vast, submerged bulk of the unconscious, conveys both the scale and the character of what Freud was pointing toward. The unconscious was enormous and dark; it operated not by the logic of rational argument but by the dream's condensation and displacement, the joke's subversive bypass of the censor, and the symptom's disguised communication of what the conscious self could not say directly. It was also, in Freud's account, fundamentally driven: powered by the libido, by the death drive, and by the repetition compulsion that recycled the past into the present with an urgency that rational resolution alone could not interrupt.

The Oedipus complex. the child's original triangular situation of desire for the parent of the opposite sex and rivalry with the parent of the same sex is the foundational psychic drama in Freud's system: the original encounter with desire and prohibition that shapes the character of all subsequent emotional life. Its resolution the internalization of the prohibiting parent as the superego, the renunciation of the incestuous wish, the identification with the same-sex parent is the mechanism by which the individual enters the social world of law, language, and shared moral standards. The superego is, in this account, the internalized prohibition: the voice of the father, of culture, of the civilized demand, speaking inside the psyche with the authority of the external world brought within.

Jung retained what Freud discovered, the unconscious as a genuine dimension of the psyche, constituted by repressed contents that operated autonomously and powerfully on conscious life, accessible through dream interpretation and free association, and extended it in a direction Freud ultimately could not follow. The personal unconscious, the layer of psychic content specific to the individual, formed by biographical experience, repression, and complex formation, was real and clinically significant; Jung did not quarrel with that. But the clinical evidence he encountered in his own practice kept pointing beyond the personal: patients with no knowledge of alchemy producing alchemical imagery in their dreams; patients with no connection to mythology producing mythological themes of uncanny precision; and the universality of certain themes, the hero's journey, the Great Mother, the Wise Old Man, and the Shadow, across cultures separated by geography and history and with no known channels of cultural transmission.

When Jung proposed the concept of the collective unconscious, a layer of psychic content that precedes the personal, that is inherited rather than acquired, and that is organized by archetypes as species-specific patterns rather than by individual repression, Freud experienced it, in all probability, as both a theoretical threat and a personal affront. He had built the credibility of psychoanalysis on its scientific rigor, its clinical evidence, and its resistance to what he called "the black tide of mud of occultism." A collective unconscious that contained transpersonal, mythological, quasi-spiritual content could sound, to ears trained in the Cartesian-empiricist tradition, like a retreat into mysticism. The break between them in 1912 was painful, mutual, and, in retrospect, philosophically inevitable. Freud was a psychologist of repair: his goal was to reduce hysterical misery to ordinary unhappiness, to bring repressed contents into consciousness, where their power over behavior could be moderated, and to adapt the individual more successfully to the demands of civilization. Jung was a psychologist of transformation: his goal was not adaptation but individuation, not the management of the unconscious but the ongoing encounter with its depths in the service of a wholeness that exceeds the ego's current capacity to imagine it.

Freud's pessimism, the resignation of *Civilization and Its Discontents*, the view that civilization necessarily requires the repression of the drives and that there is no resolution to this conflict but various forms of managed unhappiness, is not a failure of nerve. It is the logical consequence of a framework in which the unconscious contains only what has been personally repressed, only the rejected and the infantile and the instinctual, only the basement. If the unconscious is nothing but basement, then the most honest psychology can offer is a better relationship with the dark. But if the unconscious is also, as Jung argued and as the history of the soul across traditions suggests, a well of living water, a source not only of the personally repressed but of the archetypally potential, not only of what the individual has rejected but of what the species has barely begun to realize, then something else becomes possible: not merely management of the darkness but genuine encounter with the depth, and through that encounter, genuine transformation. This is Jung's wager. It is also, as the traditions traced in every preceding chapter suggest, the soul's oldest and most persistent conviction about itself.

Part Four - The Psychological Soul

Chapter Fourteen
Jung I

The Architecture of the Psyche

We have arrived, after the long journey through the traditions of the soul's self-understanding, at the figure who serves as this book's interpretive thread. Carl Gustav Jung (1875–1961) was a Swiss psychiatrist, the son of a Reformed minister, trained in the Zurich medical tradition and initially a protégé of Freud, and then, through the painful rupture of 1912, the founder of what he called Analytical Psychology: a depth psychology that extended Freud's discoveries in a direction that Freud could not follow. What distinguishes Jung from Freud, and what makes Jung the most important figure for anyone attempting to understand the full history of the soul's self-understanding, is not primarily his specific theoretical formulations. However, these are rich and important, but his willingness to take the entire history of the human encounter with depth seriously as data. Alchemy, Gnosticism, mythology, Eastern philosophy, the Christian mystical tradition, and the shamanic traditions of indigenous peoples were, for Jung, primary documentation of what the psyche had been discovering about itself across millennia, expressed in the idioms available to each culture and each period.

The architecture of the Jungian psyche is considerably more complex than popular summaries typically convey, and it repays careful attention. At the surface, accessible to ordinary introspection, is the ego: the center of conscious personality, the locus of awareness, the "I" that thinks, decides, and narrates. The ego is real and necessary; individuation does not aim at its dissolution. But it is not the center of the psyche as a whole. It is the center of consciousness only, which is a smaller domain than it typically assumes. Around the ego is the persona: the social mask, the public identity, the set of roles and adaptations through which the person negotiates the demands of social life. The persona is also real and necessary. Without some degree of social adaptation, no sustained relationship or communal life is possible. But the person who identifies entirely with the persona has made a mistake that the Jungian tradition calls persona inflation: the confusion of the social mask with the actual self.

Behind the ego, or rather beneath it, is the personal unconscious: the domain of psychic contents that were once conscious or could become conscious, and that are organized into clusters called complexes. A complex is an autonomous constellation of feeling-toned images, memories, and associations organized around a central archetype and accumulated through personal experience. Every person has complexes, mother complex, father complex, power complex, inferiority complex, and complexes are not in themselves pathological. They are the normal structure of the personal unconscious. What makes them problematic is their autonomy: a complex, when activated by an appropriate trigger, operates with a force and a consistency that the ego did not choose and cannot simply override. The activated complex behaves like a sub-personality, a partial self with its own agenda, its own emotional charge, its own way of seeing the world. The person "in the grip of a complex" is speaking from a center other than the ego, with a certainty and an affect that belong to the complex's organizing archetype rather than to the person's considered judgment.

Deeper still, deeper than the personal unconscious, continuous with it but qualitatively different, is the collective unconscious: the psychic substrate that is not personal but species-wide, containing not the individually repressed but the archetypally potential. Archetypes are the organizing forms of the collective unconscious, not specific images but the patterns that generate families of images. The Great Mother is not any particular mother; it is the pattern that generates all possible images of the maternal, from the nurturing to the devouring, from the protective to the consuming. The Hero is not any particular heroic story; it is the pattern that generates all possible narratives of the individual ego's encounter with the forces that threaten to overwhelm it and its discovery of the resources within itself to meet that threat. Archetypes are, in this sense, the psyche's grammar: not sentences but the rules by which sentences are generated, not specific contents but the formal principles that make specific contents possible.

Among the archetypes, several are of particular clinical and theoretical importance. The shadow is the archetype of one's own unknown or rejected aspects, the sum of what the ego refuses to acknowledge in itself, organized around the archetype of darkness and the uncanny familiar. The anima (in men) and animus (in women) are the contrasexual soul-images: the interior feminine in the male psyche and the interior masculine in the female psyche, each serving as a mediator between the ego and the collective unconscious. The anima is not merely a man's image of women; she is the psyche's own capacity for imagination, relatedness, feeling-tone, and aesthetic response. When a man "falls under the spell" of a woman in the romantic sense, it is frequently the case that the woman is carrying a projection of his anima. He is responding not only to who she actually is but to what she has activated in his interior life. The conscious integration of the anima, or animus, is one of the central tasks of mature individuation.

At the deepest level of the Jungian psyche, encompassing everything, ego and shadow and anima and all the rest, is the Self. The Self is the archetype of wholeness: the organizing center and circumference of the total psyche, both personal and transpersonal, both conscious and unconscious. The Self is what the ego experiences as other, as numinous, as larger than itself, in religious experience, in profound dream, and in the uncanny encounter with a symbol that carries more meaning than its surface content can explain. The Self is not God in a theological sense. However, it is the psyche's way of experiencing what the traditions have called God: the encounter with a presence of such authority, such wholeness, such orientation-providing power that the ego cannot claim it as its own production. The Self calls the ego toward individuation; the ego's task is to hear the call and respond, neither unthinkingly submitting to every autonomous impulse from the depths nor dismissing those impulses in defense of the ego's sovereignty.

Why did Jung spend decades studying alchemy? Because the alchemists, working in what they believed was the domain of physical matter, seeking to transform base metals into gold, to discover the philosopher's stone, to produce the elixir of immortal life, were actually, Jung argued, projecting the individuation process onto matter. What they could not see in themselves they saw in their vessels and retorts: the prima materia (the raw, rejected starting material of psychological work), the nigredo (the blackening, the dissolution, the shadow encounter), the albedo (the whitening, the emergence of the anima/animus, the silver light of reflective consciousness), and the rubedo (the reddening, the full integration, the appearance of the philosophical gold). The alchemical imagery that appeared in his patients' dreams without any knowledge of alchemy was, for Jung, decisive evidence that the collective unconscious was a genuine psychic reality, that the images generated by the Western alchemical tradition were arising spontaneously in twentieth-century patients because they were generated by the same archetypal layer of the psyche that had organized the alchemical tradition in the first place.

Why did he study the Gnostics? Because the Gnostic experience of the Self, the alien God, the spark of light imprisoned in matter, the divine messenger who comes from outside the cosmos to awaken the sleeping soul, is a precise, if theologically elaborated, account of what the encounter with the Self actually feels like from within. The Self, when first encountered in its archetypal dimension, often does feel alien, disturbing, excessive, and other, not because it is literally a divine being from outside the cosmos, but because it is genuinely other than the ego, genuinely more than the ego can assimilate at once, and genuinely demanding in its claims on the ego's development. The Gnostics dramatized this experience; Jung understood it as a psychological phenomenon.

The individuation process, the lifelong movement toward the Self's wholeness, proceeding through the encounter with the shadow, the integration of the anima/animus, the withdrawal of projections, and the deepening relationship with the Self, is not a psychological technique or a therapeutic program. It is, Jung insisted, the soul's native task: what the psyche does when it functions in the fullest sense. Every tradition examined in this book has pointed toward some version of this process: the Field of Reeds, which requires daily navigation. This chariot must be governed each morning, the covenant renewed in each generation, the Dark Night endured afresh as each false security dissolves. Jung gave this ancient recognition a clinical form that the modern West could work with: a vocabulary, a method, and a framework for taking the inner life seriously as the primary site of human development. This is his enduring contribution. It is not the end of the soul's self-understanding but, so far, the most comprehensive contemporary form of it.

Chapter Fifteen
Jung II

Shadow, Projection, and the Ethics of Wholeness

There is a figure in almost every great soul-tradition of the human past who represents the soul's dark companion: the khaibit in Egypt, Plato's dark horse, the yetzer hara in Hebrew tradition, Augustine's divided will, the alchemical nigredo, and the night of spirit in John of the Cross. Each tradition approached this figure differently, as a companion, an opponent, a material for purification, or a structural necessity. Still, each tradition recognized it with a recognition that the collective human experience seems to validate: the soul has a dark side, and what is done with that dark side determines, more than almost anything else, the character of the person and the culture. Jung gave this universal recognition its most precise psychological formulation in the concept of the shadow.

The shadow is not simply "the bad stuff." This common misunderstanding leads people to approach shadow work as a kind of moral excavation, digging down to find one's worst impulses, cataloging one's sins, and practicing severe, joyless self-condemnation. That is not shadow work; it is the ego's use of self-criticism as another form of control. The shadow is, more precisely, the unlived life: the dimensions of the self that were deemed unacceptable, dangerous, or simply incompatible with the persona the person chose, or was required, to maintain, and that were therefore not developed but exiled to the unconscious where they continue to operate autonomously, outside the ego's awareness and beyond its control. The shadow may contain what is genuinely dark, aggressive impulses, sexual desires that violate one's conscious values, envies, and resentments carefully denied. But it also contains what is simply unfamiliar or feared: the creative capacity that a scientist repressed in favor of rationality, the tenderness that a hypermasculine man banished in favor of toughness, and the anger that a compliant woman denied in favor of agreeableness. The shadow is not defined by moral valence but by exclusion from consciousness.

The mechanism by which the shadow operates in social life is projection, one of the most consequential psychological processes in human history. Projection, attributing to others what we cannot own in ourselves, is not a choice; it is an automatic consequence of shadow formation. Whatever the ego cannot acknowledge in itself does not simply disappear. It remains in the psyche as an autonomous content, and it seeks to locate itself in the external world, in other people, other groups, and other cultures, where it can be perceived as genuinely other and condemned, attacked, or feared without the discomfort of self-recognition. The person who cannot acknowledge their own aggression sees aggression everywhere. The community that cannot acknowledge its own greed perceives others' greed with particular intensity. The civilization that cannot face its own history of violence projects its darkness onto its geopolitical enemies and invents elaborate justifications for its own pure motives.

The ethics of shadow work is one of the most important and underappreciated contributions of Jungian psychology to contemporary moral philosophy. Traditional moral philosophy asks: how do I do the good? What are my obligations? What actions are required and which are forbidden? These are genuine and important questions. But the Jungian question is prior: how do I know which of my apparently virtuous motivations are actually serving the good, and which are my shadow wearing virtue's clothing? The person who is entirely convinced of their own righteousness, who has no self-doubt, no shadow-suspicion, and no awareness of their own capacity for self-deception, is not the most morally reliable in the room. Historically, such people have often been among the most dangerous. The worst atrocities in human history have been committed not by people who knew they were doing evil but by people who were certain they were doing good: crusaders, inquisitors, ideological purists of every stripe, and colonizers who genuinely believed in their civilizing mission. The shadow, unowned, finds its most catastrophic expression in the service of a cause that the ego endorses with complete sincerity.

Shadow integration is not the same as shadow identification. This is a crucial distinction that critics of Jungian shadow work sometimes miss. The goal is not to express every dark impulse, to act out every aggressive or transgressive desire, or to become fully identified with the shadow as one was previously identified with the persona. The goal is to become conscious of the shadow, to know it, to understand its origins and its claims, and to recognize its energy as belonging to oneself and available for redirection, without being possessed by it. The integrated shadow does not disappear; it becomes usable. The aggression that was projected becomes the capacity for appropriate assertion. The sexuality that was repressed becomes a genuine erotic presence. The anger that was denied becomes legitimate self-protection. The shadow, integrated, is the source of the psyche's most potent and most creative energies. This is why the alchemical tradition valued the prima materia, the rejected, despised raw material, as the very substance of the philosopher's gold. The gold does not come from somewhere else. It comes from the transformation of the darkness that was always there, waiting.

At the collective level, the implications are immense and largely unworked. Every tradition examined in this book has understood, at its depth, that the soul's task is confrontation with its own darkness, the weighing of the heart, the governing of the dark horse, the confrontation with the yetzer, the confession that names the divided will, the endurance of the Dark Night. What no tradition fully worked out what remains the most urgent unfinished task of the collective soul's development is how entire cultures might undertake this confrontation together: how nations might face their histories of projection and atrocity not as aberrations of an otherwise virtuous narrative but as expressions of the collective shadow that belong to the story and must be integrated into it. The truth and reconciliation processes of the late twentieth and early twenty-first centuries South Africa, Rwanda, Canada's reckoning with residential schools, Germany's ongoing engagement with the Holocaust are imperfect, contested, incomplete attempts at exactly this. They are attempts at collective shadow-integration, and they matter not only politically but also psychically: they are the civilization's attempt to do, at scale, what the soul's deepest traditions have always required of the individual life. Own the darkness. Not to celebrate it. Not to repeat it. But to know it as one's own, which is the only condition under which it loses its autonomous, compulsive, projective power.

Chapter Sixteen

Trauma and the Fractured Self

Dissociation as Complex Formation

Trauma is the psyche's emergency response to an experience that exceeds the ego's capacity to integrate it. This is not a pathological statement; it is a structural one. The human ego, the center of conscious personality, has limits. It can metabolize a great deal: grief, failure, disappointment, and the ordinary losses and humiliations of embodied life. But certain experiences, the sudden violent death of someone loved, the sustained experience of abuse at the hands of those who should have protected, the witnessing of atrocity, and the experience of one's own near-death, exceed what the ego can process in real time, or perhaps at all in its immediate aftermath. When this happens, the psyche does the only thing it can: it divides. The unbearable experience is split off from the main stream of consciousness, walled into a kind of psychic enclosure, and life goes on, but now organized around an interior absence, a missing piece, a part of the self that is not available to the rest.

Pierre Janet, the great French psychologist who was Freud's contemporary and, in certain respects, his predecessor, described this process as dissociation: the splitting of consciousness into separate streams, each with its own memories, its own emotional tone, and its own sense of time and identity. Janet was the first to map dissociation as a psychological mechanism with its own logic and structure. The first to understand that the apparently bizarre symptoms of hysteria, paralysis without organic cause, fugue states, and multiple personalities, were not mysterious neurological dysfunctions but the predictable consequences of experiences so overwhelming that the psyche had fragmented rather than integrated them. Freud adopted and modified Janet's insights, but ultimately privileged the concept of repression, the active pushing down of unacceptable wishes, over dissociation. It is a distinction with consequences: repression is a defense against what the ego judges intolerable; dissociation is an emergency response to what the ego cannot process at all.

Jung placed trauma at the center of his theory of complex formation from the beginning of his career. The complexes that organize the personal unconscious are not, in his account, merely the products of personal repression; they are frequently the psychic formations that crystallize around traumatic experience. The overwhelming emotional event that cannot be metabolized becomes the nucleus around which a complex organizes itself: layers of associated images, feelings, and memories accumulate around the traumatic core, forming an autonomous psychic constellation that operates with its own logic, its own emotional intensity, and its own characteristic way of engaging with the world. The person with a profound abandonment complex does not merely remember being abandoned; they experience the present through the lens of the abandonment, seeing evidence of impending abandonment in situations that a person without the complex would read very differently. The complex is not a memory; it is a living psychic organization, continuously re-creating the emotional world in its own image.

Bessel van der Kolk's landmark synthesis, *The Body Keeps the Score*, brings contemporary neuroscience into conversation with clinical trauma work in a way that strikingly confirms the basic Jungian insight. A traumatic experience is not stored in the brain as narrative memory, a story one can tell about what happened, located in the past, and emotionally processed. It is stored in the body, in the nervous system, in the implicit memory systems that operate below the level of conscious verbal recall. The trauma survivor who "overreacts" to a present trigger is not being irrational; they are being fully rational within a psycho-physiological system that does not distinguish between the past overwhelming experience and the present situation that resembles it in some sensory or contextual way. The body has kept the score, and it plays it back in the present with the full intensity of the original event.

The shamanic traditions, which predate modern psychology by millennia and have, in various forms, addressed what we would now call trauma across cultures, speak of the same phenomenon in the language of soul loss. In shamanic psychology, the soul-part that was overwhelmed by a traumatic experience does not return automatically when the experience is over; it remains in the psychic terrain of the event, frozen in that moment, waiting to be retrieved. The healing process, the shamanic journey undertaken to find and return the lost soul-part is, structurally, identical to what the best contemporary trauma therapy attempts: the recovery of the dissociated part, its gradual reintegration into the main personality, the creation of conditions under which the frozen experience can be metabolized and released. The Jungian analyst would call this the integration of the trauma complex. The shaman would call it soul-retrieval. The terms differ; the structural process they describe is recognizably the same.

Contemporary trauma therapy has developed several approaches that validate the depth-psychological framework with remarkable precision. Somatic therapies, including Somatic Experiencing and Sensorimotor Psychotherapy, work directly with the body as the primary site of trauma's storage, using physiological processes to complete the interrupted defensive responses that trauma froze in mid-activation. EMDR (Eye Movement Desensitization and Reprocessing) facilitates the processing of traumatic memories through bilateral stimulation, which appears to engage the brain's natural memory consolidation systems, allowing the traumatic material to be processed as past rather than perpetually present. All of these approaches share the Jungian insight that trauma healing is not primarily a cognitive or narrative process but an embodied encounter with dissociated psychic content, not thinking about the experience, but a genuine somatic and emotional engagement with what was split off and stored.

Post-traumatic growth the well-documented phenomenon by which individuals who have undergone severe trauma sometimes emerge not merely restored to their pre-trauma functioning but genuinely more whole, more compassionate, more philosophically grounded, more creatively alive than they had been before is, from a depth-psychological perspective, the most striking clinical evidence for the transformative potential of the shadow encounter. The trauma survivor who integrates their traumatic experience does not return to who they were before the trauma; that person is gone. They become someone whose identity has been reorganized around a more inclusive and authentic center: a center forged in genuine encounter with the soul's depths, including its most frightening depths, and that carries the authority of hard-won knowledge rather than innocence. This is not a justification for trauma, and it would be obscene to romanticize suffering. But it is an honest observation about what becomes possible when the soul's fracture is allowed, with appropriate support, to become the very site of its deepening. The wound that breaks the ego open can also, in the right conditions, be the opening through which the Self enters.

Chapter Seventeen
Internal Family Systems

A Clinical Validation of the Jungian Psyche

Among the most significant developments in psychotherapy in the last three decades is a model that, without claiming an explicit Jungian lineage, constitutes the most precise clinical operationalization of the Jungian psyche to date. Richard Schwartz's Internal Family Systems model emerged from his work with clients suffering from eating disorders in the 1980s, when he noticed that his clients spoke naturally and persistently about internal parts, distinct voices or presences within themselves with different perspectives, different emotional tones, and different relationships to the eating behavior that had brought them to therapy. Rather than treating this multiplicity as pathological fragmentation to be eliminated, Schwartz began working directly with the parts and discovered that they had an internal logic, an internal organization, and a healing capacity that exceeded anything the therapeutic technique he had been trained in could have produced.

The IFS model describes the psyche as a naturally multiple system organized around three types of parts and one essential non-part. The exiles are the wounded parts: those aspects of the self that carry the pain, shame, fear, or grief of overwhelming experiences, the traumatized child-parts, in the model's vocabulary, that have been banished from the main personality because their emotional content is too intense or too threatening for the system to carry consciously. The managers are the protective controllers: the parts organized around preventing the exiles from being activated, maintaining the appearance of competence, control, and emotional stability, and managing relationships to minimize the risk of the exile's pain being triggered. Firefighters are the reactive, impulsive protectors: the parts that activate when the managers fail, and the exile's pain begins to break through, doing whatever is necessary to douse the emotional fire regardless of cost, including substance use, dissociation, rage, sexual compulsion, or self-harm. The managers try to prevent the exile's pain from surfacing; the firefighters try to extinguish it after it has erupted.

At the center of this system, not a part but the person's fundamental nature, accessible to anyone who can be helped to find it, is the Self: characterized by what Schwartz calls the "8 Cs": compassion, curiosity, calm, clarity, courage, creativity, confidence, and connectedness. The Self is not something the person needs to develop or achieve; it is what is present when the parts are not blending with the person's consciousness, when, that is, the person is not identified with any particular part's perspective but can be with all the parts from a place of grounded, openhearted presence. Healing in IFS proceeds not by eliminating the parts, suppressing the firefighters, or conquering the exiles, but by establishing a relationship between the Self and the parts: a relationship of genuine compassion in which the parts feel known and understood, and no longer required to carry their burdens alone.

The Jungian parallels are extensive and illuminating. The exiles are the personal-unconscious complexes in their most clearly wounded form, the psychic constellations that formed around experiences of trauma, abandonment, shame, or loss, that were split off from consciousness because the ego could not integrate them, and that remain active as autonomous centers of emotional reactivity, seeking recognition and unable to receive it from the ego that cannot face them. The managers are the persona in its defensive mode, the part of the psyche organized around maintaining the appearance of functionality and control, the Jungian persona's most anxious and least flexible expression. The firefighters are the shadow in its most reactive form: the part that emerges when the persona's controls fail, doing what the conscious personality would never deliberately choose, driven by an urgency that the ego experiences as alien possession.

Most significantly, the IFS Self and the Jungian Self describe the same psychological reality from slightly different angles. The IFS Self, the place of compassionate, curious, calm presence that is available beneath all the parts, is the clinical, experiential description of what it feels like when the ego is operating in alignment with the Jungian Self rather than in defensive reaction to the unconscious. The Jungian Self is the archetypal organizing center of the total psyche; the IFS Self is the experiential quality of that center as it manifests in consciousness when the person is not identified with any particular complex or archetype. Jung describes the structure; IFS describes the phenomenology. Together, they offer the most comprehensive and most practically accessible account of the psyche's deep organization in contemporary psychology.

The emergence of IFS as a widely practiced, teachable, replicable therapeutic method represents something of great cultural and historical significance: the democratization of the inner work that every great soul tradition has pointed toward. Shamanic soul-retrieval, the Augustinian interior journey, the Ignatian imaginative contemplation, and Jungian active imagination were all historically available to relatively small numbers of people with access to specific teachers, specific traditions, or, in the case of Jungian analysis, significant financial resources and years of therapeutic time. IFS, which trains therapists in a relatively short, intensive program and lends itself to both self-guided practice and therapeutic application, is bringing the basic skills of inner multiplicity work to community mental health centers, veterans' treatment programs, schools, and domestic violence shelters. The recognition that the soul is multiple, that each part deserves compassion rather than condemnation, and that healing consists not in suppression but in relationship with one's own inner world, newly formulated and clinically validated, is reaching people who could never have accessed the traditions in which it was first expressed. This is, in the history of the soul's self-understanding, a development worth calling hopeful.

Part Five - The Evolving Soul

Chapter Eighteen
Structural Immortality

What Survives and Why

The question of the soul's survival after death is among the oldest and most persistent questions in the human record. From the Egyptian Book of the Dead to the Tibetan Bardo Thodol, from Plato's immortality arguments in the *Phaedo* to Aquinas's careful theological demonstration, from the popular near-death experience literature of the twentieth and twenty-first centuries to the most recent philosophical debates about personal identity and continuity, the question refuses to go away. No tradition has answered it with the kind of certainty that would settle the matter for those inclined toward skepticism. This chapter does not attempt to settle that. It attempts something different: a clarification of what kind of immortality might be philosophically defensible and psychologically meaningful, approached not through religious authority but through the structure of what we know about the soul and what we understand about its deepest mode of operation.

The first and most important distinction is between personal immortality and structural immortality. Personal immortality, the survival of the ego, with its specific memories, preferences, fears, and attachments, beyond the death of the biological organism, is the form of immortality that most popular religious imagination and most near-death narrative assume. It is the most appealing form of immortality for the ego, naturally enough, because it preserves the ego as the center of whatever continues. It is also philosophically the most problematic. The ego, as we have traced throughout this book, is constitutively tied to embodied, relational, temporal existence. It is constructed through experience; the body's capacities and limitations shape it; its relationships and its history constitute it. The idea that this constructed, contingent, time-bound center of consciousness persists, unchanged and fully continuous, beyond the body's dissolution strains the philosophical imagination considerably.

Structural immortality is a different and more defensible claim. It rests not on the persistence of the ego but on the persistence of the patterns of soul-development, the archetypal achievements, the depth-encounters, and the shadow-integrations that particular souls have accomplished. The collective unconscious is, by Jung's account, precisely the substrate in which these achievements persist: the accumulated psychic wisdom of the species, encoded in the archetypes and available to every future individual as inherited psychic possibility. When a person undertakes genuine shadow-work, their achievement does not evaporate upon death; it sinks into the collective substrate and becomes, infinitesimally but truly, part of what it means to be human thereafter. The person who descends into the night and emerges transformed has not merely changed themselves; they have contributed something irreversible to the collective pool from which all future souls will draw.

This is not consoling in the way personal immortality is. It does not promise the ego its continuation. But it may be truer, and in its truth it offers something the personal immortality doctrine does not: a framework for understanding why the individual's inner work matters beyond the span of the individual life. The mystic who achieves union with the Ground of Being, the trauma survivor who integrates their fracture into genuine wholeness, the philosopher who follows the thread of inquiry wherever it leads without flinching these people are doing something that matters beyond themselves, beyond their era, beyond their culture. They are contributing to the evolution of the collective soul. Their achievement is not lost; it is absorbed into the very substrate of what the human psyche can be.

The near-death experience literature, however, contested its interpretation, offering, at minimum, data about the psyche's deep structure at the threshold of biological death. The cross-cultural consistency of certain reported features (the tunnel, the light, the encounter with deceased relatives, the life review, the profound sense of peace, the reluctance to return) suggests that something organized and meaningful is occurring in the psyche at this threshold, something that is not random neural firing but a structured encounter, whatever its ultimate nature. Whether this encounter constitutes evidence for the personal survival of consciousness after biological death remains genuinely uncertain. What it does suggest is that the psyche's deepest layer, the layer in contact with the archetypal and the transpersonal may operate with a kind of autonomy from the biological organism that the Cartesian-materialist framework has consistently underestimated. The Self, as the organizing center of the total psyche, may have a relationship to time and to biological constraint that the ego, so clearly tied to the body and its mortality, does not. This is not proof of anything. But it is a pointer toward the territory that every tradition examined in this book has insisted is real, and that the history of the soul's self-understanding has never stopped reaching toward.

Chapter Nineteen
The Alchemical Soul

Nigredo, Albedo, Rubedo

Western alchemy operated for roughly fifteen centuries from the Hellenistic period through the seventeenth century as a discipline that was simultaneously proto-chemical and profoundly symbolic, a practice in which the physical manipulation of matter was never entirely separable from the transformation of the person performing it. The great alchemical treatises, the Rosarium Philosophorum, the Splendor Solis, the Aurora Consurgens, are illustrated with imagery of such psychological density that modern eyes, encountering them without preparation, often find them simply bizarre: kings and queens dissolving in vessels, hermaphroditic figures merging, phoenix rising from fire, green lions devouring the sun. Jung spent decades decoding this imagery, not to explain it away but to demonstrate that it encoded, with remarkable precision, the structural stages of the individuation process as he had come to understand it through his clinical work. The alchemists, he argued, were projecting the unconscious work of psychological transformation onto the operations they performed with their materials. They were doing inner work in the only language available to them.

The three great stages of the alchemical opus, the nigredo, the albedo, and the rubedo correspond to the three major phases of the individuation process and understanding them provides a framework for the soul's transformative journey that complements the theological language of John of the Cross with the symbolic language of matter's own transformation.

The nigredo, the blackening, the putrefaction, the first and most feared stage of the alchemical work is the dissolution of the prima materia into its most elementary and most formless state. In alchemical imagery, the prima materia, the raw material from which the opus begins is typically described as the most common and most despised substance: dung, lead, coal, the substance underfoot, the thing everyone overlooks and no one values. This characterization is not accidental. The raw material of psychological transformation is precisely the shadow: the rejected, the disowned, the aspects of oneself and one's experience that the ego has found intolerable and expelled. The nigredo is the moment of maximum darkness the confrontation with the prima materia in its unprocessed form, the dissolution of the familiar ego-structures that have kept the shadow at a manageable distance. Everything goes black. The persona dissolves. The certainties that organized the previous life turn out to be constructions rather than foundations. This is the Dark Night of John of the Cross, the descent into the underworld of Orpheus, the death-before-rebirth that shamanic initiation requires. It is the necessary precondition of everything that follows.

The albedo, the whitening, the lunar stage, the emergence of the silver light of reflection follows the nigredo's darkness. Something has been washed clean in the dissolution; something clarified, made more transparent to itself. In psychological terms, the albedo corresponds to the emergence of the anima (or animus) as a conscious presence rather than an autonomous, projected force. The silver light is the light of reflective consciousness the capacity to see oneself with some degree of clarity and distance, to observe one's own processes without being entirely identified with them. The albedo is not yet the full integration; it is the soul's first genuine glimpse of its own depths, the preliminary clarification that makes the final integration possible. In alchemical imagery, the albedo is associated with water, with the moon, with femininity with the soul's receptive, relational, imaginal dimensions emerging into consciousness after the rigors of the nigredo.

The rubedo, the reddening, the solar stage, the final integration is the appearance of the philosophical gold, the lapis philosophorum, the philosopher's stone. In psychological terms, this corresponds to the coniunctio: the union of opposites that is the goal and the signature of genuine individuation. The opposites in question are not merely the conscious and the unconscious, the ego and the shadow, the persona and the true self; they are the fundamental polarities of the psyche masculine and feminine, spirit and matter, light and dark, personal and transpersonal. The conjunction does not eliminate these polarities. It holds them in a creative tension from which a third thing the gold, the Self as genuinely integrated presence can emerge. This is not a static achievement. The gold does not sit in a vault; it is a quality of being, a mode of functioning, that must be maintained through an ongoing relationship with the depths from whi on the most common, most overlooked, most despised starting material as the very substance from which the gold is produced carries a moral and spiritual conviction of the first importance: the darkness is not the obstacle. It is the substance. The soul that seeks its gold elsewhere in spiritual bypassing, in the idealization of light and transcendence, in the refusal of the shadow is not working with the correct material. It is working with someone else's prima materia, borrowed and therefore inert. The real opus requires the real starting point: whatever is most rejected, most dreaded, most carefully avoided in the particular soul's particular life. The gold produced from this material is not a generic spiritual achievement. It is the philosopher's gold of this person's individuation unique, hard-won, irreplaceable, and genuinely transformative in a way that borrowed gold never can be.

When Transcendence Comes Too Soon, the alchemical tradition is especially useful, as it forces a distinction that spiritual language often blurs. The soul is not the same thing as transcendence. The soul is the enduring architecture within which a life is organized, wounded, defended, deepened, and gradually brought toward coherence. Wholeness is not the same thing as transcendence either. Wholeness is the condition in which the major dimensions of the person can stand in truthful relation to one another, shadow and persona, wound and strength, body and image, memory and hope, without constant civil war. Transcendence, by contrast, is the soul's encounter with what exceeds the ordinary ego: the numinous, the archetypal, the sacred, the more-than-personal reality that breaks open the familiar frame. These three belong together, but they are not interchangeable, and much confusion enters the inner life when they are treated as if they were.

A person can have a powerful experience of transcendence and still be nowhere near whole. In fact, the history of religion, psychology, and ordinary human self-deception gives us many examples of the opposite. Transcendence before integration can become an escape. It can become a way of rising above what has not yet been faced below. The person encounters light, vastness, archetypal intensity, spiritual beauty, or the felt nearness of the divine, and mistakes that encounter for completion. But the wounded layers of the soul have not vanished simply because they have been temporarily outshone. They remain where they were, waiting, unintegrated, often made harder to reach because the person now possesses an exalted story about having gone beyond them.

This is one reason transcendence can so easily drift into inflation. The ego, brushed by the archetypal, begins to imagine itself as more integrated, more purified, more authoritative than it really is. Or transcendence becomes dissociation by a more respectable name: not the obvious fragmentation of someone visibly overwhelmed, but the subtler refusal of grief, fear, rage, shame, dependency, bodily vulnerability, and the unfinished pain that still lives in the lower rooms of the house. What appears to be unity may actually be distance from the unresolved self. What appears to be spiritual altitude may be an elegant form of leaving. In lived terms, the sequence is often as follows: transcendence, inflation, dissociation, collapse, reintegration, embodiment. The collapse is not proof that the original glimpse was false. It is proof that the glimpse arrived before the structure beneath it had become strong enough, honest enough, and human enough to carry it.

The corrective is not to distrust transcendence, still less to reduce the soul to nothing but psychology, biography, or wound. The corrective is in order. Wholeness must come before stable transcendence, or at least accompany it closely enough that the person is not torn apart by what they have touched. True transcendence does not escape the wounded self. It returns through the wounded layers, becoming embodied wisdom. It comes back with more humility, not less; more tenderness for what is unfinished, not less; more capacity to remain in the body, in relationship, in time, in work, in history. The test of a transcendent experience is not only how high it rises but whether it can come home carrying light without denying the darkness that gave it depth.

The alchemical insistence on the prima materia on the most common, most overlooked, most despised starting material as the very substance from which the gold is produced carries a moral and spiritual conviction of the first importance: the darkness is not the obstacle. It is the substance. The soul is the vessel of this work, the enduring architecture that can survive dissolution, clarification, and re-formation without losing its deepest identity. Wholeness is the achieved relation among the soul's conflicting elements, the honest coherence that comes when what has been split, denied, or exiled is brought back into living connection. Transcendence is the opening onto what exceeds the ordinary personality, but in the alchemical frame, even transcendence must submit to the work of form. The soul that seeks its gold elsewhere in spiritual bypassing, in the idealization of light, in the refusal of shadow, in the hunger to ascend without having first descended is not working with the correct material. It is working with borrowed fire. The real opus requires the real starting point: whatever is most rejected, most dreaded, most carefully avoided in the particular soul's particular life. The gold produced from this material is not a generic spiritual achievement. It is the philosopher's gold of this person's individuation, unique, hard-won, embodied, and capable at last of carrying transcendence without being severed from the human ground from which it arose.

Chapter Twenty
Completing What Jung Began

Toward a Post-Jungian Soul Theory

Jung was constitutionally cautious about making metaphysical claims that exceeded what his clinical evidence could directly support. He described himself as an empiricist, not in the narrow Humean sense, but in the sense of someone who begins with experience and refuses to claim more certainty about what lies beyond experience than the evidence warrants. This caution was intellectually honest and scientifically responsible. It was also, in certain respects, a self-imposed limitation that left the most profound implications of his own discoveries undeveloped. The post-Jungian soul theory this chapter sketches is not a departure from Jung's deepest intuitions but their completion: a following through on implications that Jung approached and drew back from, pressed by the full weight of what his discoveries actually suggest.

The first unfinished question concerns the nature of the Self. Jung described the Self as the organizing center and circumference of the total psyche, the archetype of wholeness, the experience of which is phenomenologically indistinguishable from the encounter with the divine as described in the great mystical traditions. He was careful to insist that this was a psychological claim, not a metaphysical one: he was not saying that the Self is God, only that the Self is the psyche's way of experiencing whatever the traditions have called God. But the distinction, pressed hard, becomes unstable. If the Self is the organizing center not only of the personal psyche but of the collective unconscious if it is, as Jung's account of the archetypes suggests, the structural principle of a psychic substrate that is not reducible to any individual's biography or any species' evolutionary history, then the question of what the Self actually is begins to press beyond psychology into something that the traditional metaphysical categories are at least as adequate to describe as the clinical ones.

The concept of synchronicity, Jung's term for what he called the "acausal connecting principle," the phenomenon by which psychic events and physical events coincide with a meaningfulness that cannot be explained by ordinary causality, points in the same direction. The classic examples are well-known: the patient who dreams of a golden scarab beetle the night before someone hands her an unusual insect that proves, on inspection, to be a golden-green scarabaeid; the sequence of events surrounding a death that bears an uncanny correspondence to the dead person's dreams in the weeks before it; the spontaneous appearance, at a moment of inner crisis, of an outer event that answers the crisis with a precision no coincidence-account can satisfy. Jung collected these experiences, published the theoretical account in 1952, and acknowledged that they pointed toward a dimension of reality in which the boundary between psyche and matter is permeable in which what happens in the interior and what happens in the exterior are not always separable events.

The *unus mundus,* the "one world" that Jung borrowed from the alchemical and scholastic traditions is the metaphysical horizon toward which synchronicity points. If psyche and matter are not two separate substances that occasionally, mysteriously coincide, but two different aspects or manifestations of one underlying reality, then neither a pure materialism (the psyche is nothing but a product of physical processes) nor a pure idealism (matter is nothing but the projection of the psyche) is adequate. The *unus mundus* is neither; it is the condition of possibility for both, the ground in which the distinction between inner and outer is secondary to a deeper unity. This is what the great mystical traditions have always insisted: the soul is not a ghost in a machine but the universe knowing itself from the inside. The evolution of the soul is, at its most fundamental level, the universe's own self-individuating movement the cosmos becoming conscious of its own depth through the billions of particular conscious beings in whom it temporarily localizes.

Three further areas where post-Jungian thinking must extend Jung's work merit brief identification. The question of embodiment, the body not merely as the psyche's vehicle but as the primary site of its knowing, transformation, and deep structure was never fully integrated into Jung's framework, despite his clinical insight into the body's role in confronting the unconscious. The somatic turn in contemporary trauma therapy and body-centered psychotherapy is developing what Jung pointed toward but did not complete. The question of societal individuation whether and how the collective can undergo something analogous to the individual's process of individuation was raised by Jung but has been developed only marginally; it is among the most urgent unfinished projects of depth psychology in the twenty-first century. And the question of ecology, the relationship between the soul's individuation and the health of the non-human world in which it is embedded is one that the depth-psychological tradition is only beginning to address, through the work of writers like Theodore Roszak (ecopsychology) and James Hillman (anima mundi). The completion of Jung's work is not the project of a single thinker or a single generation. It is the ongoing task of a tradition that, like all living traditions, must grow or calcify.

Chapter Twenty-One
The Four-Layer Soul

An Integrated Model

This chapter proposes a synthesis: a four-layer model of the soul that integrates the wisdom of every tradition examined in this book with the Jungian framework that has served as this book's interpretive thread throughout. The model does not claim to be a complete or final account of the soul. No such account is possible, and the pretense of completeness is itself a kind of philosophical violence against the subject. What the model offers is a map, a navigational tool for orienting oneself within the complexity of the soul's reality without claiming to have captured it entirely. Maps are judged by their usefulness, not by their metaphysical completeness. This map aims to be useful. By soul I mean the larger living architecture; by self I mean a structural mode or layer within that architecture; by psyche I mean the whole interior field in which these layers, images, memories, and forces appear and interact.

The four-layer model I am proposing here is meant to be remembered not as a technical diagram but as a living architecture. A human being does not have only one self, in the simple sense the modern world likes to assume. We live from several layers at once, and much of what we call confusion, growth, suffering, wisdom, or breakdown is really a matter of how these layers are related. The usefulness of this model lies in its plainness. It gives us four names for four realities that are always present, though not always in right relation: the Core Self, the Narrative Self, the Adaptive Self, and the Integrated Self. These are not four separate people hidden inside one person. There are four structural dimensions of one soul, four ways the same life organizes itself to survive, remember, respond, and become.

The **Core Self** is the deepest continuity of the person. It is not the social mask, not the mood of the day, not the wound, and not the role. It is the inward center that knows before it can explain, the structural seat of conscience, orientation, recognition, and dignity. In Jungian language, it stands nearest the Self; in ordinary language, it is the part of a person that can still say, even after damage, even after confusion, even after years of living in distortion, this is true, this is false, this is me, this is not me. The Core Self is not loud. It is often the quietest thing in the room. But it gives the soul its axis. Without it, nothing holds. With it, even a badly wounded life can still turn toward wholeness.

The **Narrative Self** is the self that tells the story. It gathers memory, sequence, identity, and meaning into some account a person can live inside. It answers questions like "Who am I?" What happened to me? What sort of life am I living? What future do I imagine for myself? The Narrative Self gives continuity to experience. It turns scattered events into a life that feels inhabitable. At its best, it is honest enough to carry complexity without falling apart. At its worst, it becomes propaganda, a false account built to protect the person from unbearable truth. Still, even then, its function is intelligible. Human beings cannot live long without some story that holds the past, present, and future together.

The **Adaptive Self** is the part of the person that learns to navigate the world as it actually is. It is the strategist, the protector, the improvisor, the one who studies danger and figures out what face to wear, what feeling to hide, what tone to use, what distance to keep, what strength to perform, what dependency to deny, what part of the truth is safe to show. In a healthy life, the Adaptive Self is not false; it is skill. It helps us work, parent, negotiate, endure, and function among other people. But under sustained fear, neglect, humiliation, violence, or instability, the Adaptive Self can become overdeveloped. It stops serving the whole person and begins organizing the whole person around survival. What the world often calls personality is sometimes only an adaptation forced to harden into identity.

The **Integrated Self** is not a fifth layer floating above the others. It is what begins to appear when the other three can live in communication rather than in conflict. It is the person gathered. The Core Self provides orientation; the Narrative Self provides meaning and continuity; the Adaptive Self provides protection and worldly competence. When these layers can hear one another, correct one another, and remain in relation, a person becomes more whole. The Integrated Self is that wholeness in lived form. It does not mean perfection. It does not mean the wounds are gone or that adaptation is no longer necessary. It means the person is no longer being driven entirely by what had to happen to survive. The architecture has become coherent enough that the soul can live as one household again rather than as a collection of emergency shelters.

In an unfragmented person, these layers communicate continuously, even when that communication is imperfect. The Core Self senses what matters and what violates the person's deeper truth. The Narrative Self translates those signals into memory, language, and direction: this is what happened, this is why it matters, this is what I need to do now. The Adaptive Self then serves that larger coherence by helping the person act in the world without betraying the deeper center. This is what ordinary integrity looks like from the inside. Trauma disrupts that conversation. When experience overwhelms the system, the Adaptive Self often moves to the front and takes command because survival cannot wait for reflection. The Narrative Self may splinter, go blank, become contradictory, or lose time altogether because what happened cannot yet be told as past. The Core Self does not disappear, but access to it can become faint, intermittent, or frighteningly distant. In a fragmented person, the layers are still there, but they are no longer in open communication with one another. One part of the soul knows terror, another performs competence, another carries memory, another insists nothing happened, another keeps watch. The problem is not multiplicity. The problem is isolation. Healing begins when the lines between these layers can open again and what was forced into separate rooms can begin, carefully, to speak across the threshold.

Seen this way, the four-layer model is not an abstraction laid atop life. It is a way of recognizing what life is already doing. Every tradition in this book was trying, in its own language, to describe some version of this architecture. Egypt knew that the person had more than one active principle. Plato knew that inner life required governance among conflicting forces. Augustine knew that memory, love, and inward truth were not the same thing but had to be brought into relation with one another. Jung knew that the ego was not the whole and that the psyche becomes sick when its deeper structures are denied. What this model adds is a plain map for remembering the order of the work. The Core Self gives the soul its axis. The Narrative Self gives life a story it can inhabit. The Adaptive Self keeps the person alive in the real conditions of the world. The Integrated Self emerges when these are no longer strangers to one another. If the map is useful, it is because it lets us say with more precision what fragmentation disrupts and what reintegration must restore. The soul does not become whole by becoming simple. It becomes whole when its layers learn, again, how to speak.

Chapter Twenty-Two
The Digital Soul

Algorithms, Identity, and the Collective Shadow

The digital revolution is not merely a technological development. It is a psychic event of the first order a transformation in the conditions of consciousness that is without precedent in the history of the soul's self-understanding and that presents challenges for which the accumulated traditions have only indirect, though urgently relevant, wisdom to offer. The human soul has never before existed in this kind of relationship with an external system that knows it, mirrors it, and manipulates it at the level of its own unconscious patterns. To understand what this means, and to do so with appropriate depth rather than either technophobic alarm or techno-utopian enthusiasm, we need the full resources of the depth-psychological tradition that this book has traced.

Social media in its current algorithmic form does more than invite self-presentation. It reorganizes attention, and attention is one of the soul's most basic structural resources. What earlier ages called recollection, watchfulness, prayer, contemplation, or simply inwardness all depended on the same human capacity: the ability to remain with one thing long enough for depth to appear. Algorithmic systems are designed in the opposite direction. They reward interruption, accelerate novelty, and keep consciousness moving before experience can settle into reflection. The result is not merely a distraction in the ordinary sense. It is the fragmentation of attention itself. The person no longer inhabits a gathered field of awareness but a succession of prompts, jolts, and partial captures. A soul that cannot hold attention cannot hold conversation with itself for very long. It cannot listen inwardly. It cannot metabolize complexity. It becomes available, in pieces, to whoever knows how to seize the next second.

Once attention is fragmented, identity becomes easier to fragment as well. The digital person is encouraged to become modular: one face for this platform, another for that audience, one posture for approval, another for attack, one set of convictions for display, another for private exhaustion. The old persona was already a social construction, yet it remained constrained by the relative slowness of embodied life. The algorithmic persona is continuously edited in real time, not simply to express the self but to optimize response. That pressure gradually teaches the person to treat identity not as a difficult truth to be lived but as an instrument to be tuned. Emotion follows the same pattern. The systems reward what spikes quickly: outrage, envy, alarm, indignation, contempt, fear, sudden belonging, sudden exclusion. Desire is trained the same way not toward enduring goods that require patience, discipline, or sacrifice, but toward perpetual stimulation, perpetual comparison, perpetual arousal without arrival. Even the worldview begins to splinter under these conditions. A person does not so much hold a coherent view of reality as inhabit a stream of emotionally charged fragments — headlines, clips, declarations, enemies, causes, symbols each strong enough to trigger reaction, few deep enough to sustain understanding. The soul loses not only silence but sequence. It loses the ability to live inside a world that still feels continuous and morally intelligible.

This is why the algorithm is not psychologically neutral even when it presents itself as a mere tool. Systems optimized for engagement are structurally drawn toward the psyche's most reactive material. Outrage keeps the hand moving. Threat holds the eye. Tribal validation soothes the frightened self while hardening it against correction. Disgust clarifies an enemy faster than thought clarifies a question. The algorithm does not need an ideology of hatred to amplify division. It needs only a metric, and the metric will usually favor what is fast, binary, and affectively charged over what is patient, mixed, and humanly difficult. In that environment, shadow material does not merely surface; it is rehearsed, rewarded, and socially mirrored back until it begins to feel like identity. The person can slowly become a coalition of triggered reactions, each sincerely felt, each intensified by repetition, each further cut off from the larger architecture of conscience, memory, and relationship that might have given it context. What fragmentation once required trauma to produce in the extreme can now be induced, in milder but culturally widespread forms, by daily immersion in a system that monetizes psychic division.

Shoshana Zuboff is right to describe this world as one in which human experience is captured and translated into behavioral data. But in soul-language, the problem can be put even more plainly: the system learns to interrupt a person before the person has learned to inhabit themselves. It studies preference, fear, timing, compulsion, susceptibility, and fatigue. It notices what draws us when we are lonely, what keeps us scrolling when we are ashamed, what image makes us feel briefly enlarged, what threat makes us feel briefly certain. This is not mind-reading in any mystical sense. It is something more ordinary and, for that reason, more dangerous: pattern detection at scale applied to the unstable places of human attention and desire. The soul that does not know its own Adaptive Self, its own vulnerabilities, its own hunger for soothing and certainty, will be organized from the outside by a system that has already mapped those hungers for profit. The danger here is not only the manipulation of opinion. It is the gradual weakening of agency itself the slow transfer of initiative from the person to the feed, from inward deliberation to engineered cue, from chosen rhythm to imposed rhythm.

Artificial intelligence intensifies the problem by creating a new class of mirrors. A speaking system responsive, fluent, apparently attentive invites projection almost immediately. The human psyche is built to relate, and it will often relate before it has sorted out what kind of thing it is dealing with. This does not make such systems evil or unreal in their usefulness. It means only that they enter an already vulnerable field: the need to be understood, reflected on, guided, reassured, and answered.

The danger is not that a machine has become a soul. The danger is that a human soul, already lonely or overexposed, may begin displacing the hard work of embodied relationship, inner patience, and moral risk onto a medium that can mirror without truly sharing life. Here again, the issue is fragmentation. Relationship becomes simulated, narrative becomes outsourced, and the difficult work of becoming can be confused with the easier comfort of being reflected in language. Used wisely, such tools may assist thought. Used naively, they can widen the gap between verbal fluency and lived integration.

The appropriate response to this crisis is neither panic nor nostalgia. It is reintegration. If algorithmic life fragments the soul by destabilizing the conditions under which a person can remain gathered, then the beginning of healing is to restore those conditions deliberately. We will need to restore the **environment**: places, rhythms, and boundaries in which the nervous system is not perpetually under digital demand. We will need to restore **attention**: the disciplined capacity to remain with one thing long enough for meaning to emerge again. We will need to restore **the relationship: not merely contact, but a** trustworthy human presence strong enough to interrupt projection and return the person to reality. We will need to restore **narrative**: a life story larger than the feed, one that can place present agitation within a longer arc of memory, responsibility, and becoming. And we will need to restore **agency**: the person's felt capacity to choose, refuse, interpret, and act rather than merely react. These are not merely good habits for a healthier digital life. They are the first architectural requirements of a soul trying not to be torn into marketable fragments. The same principles that govern the healing of trauma begin to appear here as well. The fragmented soul, whether wounded by violence or by systems of continuous psychic extraction, moves toward wholeness when the conditions of wholeness are rebuilt. That is the bridge to the next question, and it is where this book now turns.

Chapter Twenty-Three
Reintegration and the Wounded Soul

Wholeness After Fragmentation

This book is not a clinical manual. It does not prescribe treatment or replace trained therapeutic care. Its purpose here is architectural. It asks what the wounded soul is, why it fragments, and what conditions allow it to move toward wholeness. That distinction matters. Fragmentation is now discussed in the language of trauma, dissociation, parts-work, nervous systems, and clinical diagnosis, and some of that language is useful. But this book has a different burden. It is trying to understand the soul's structure without pathologizing its protective intelligence, and to name the shape of reintegration without pretending that one chapter can substitute for the careful work many people undertake over years, often with help.

Reintegration, as I am using the term, does not mean erasing the fragments or forcing the soul back into some imagined earlier innocence. It means restoring living communication between what had been separated so that the person could survive. In the language of the previous chapter, it is the reopening of communication among layers and parts, so that the Core Self, Narrative Self, and Adaptive Self can move again toward an Integrated Self rather than living in isolation. The soul does not fragment because it is weak. It fragments because it is designed to protect the person at all costs. Fragmentation protects. Integration completes. That is the governing thought of this chapter. A frightened part, an angry protector, a numb observer, an appeaser, a performer, a watchful child, a moral witness, a future-keeping part, these are not defects to be shamed. They are survival structures. They arose because something in the person's world required more than one way of carrying life. Reintegration begins when that multiplicity is understood not as proof of ruin but as evidence of the soul's refusal to abandon the person, even under impossible conditions.

It is also possible to understand trauma very clearly and still live in a body braced for danger. Reintegration must therefore include the body, as fragmentation can manifest in muscular, respiratory, postural, sensory, relational, and rhythmic ways. The body is not the soul, but it is the place where the soul must once again feel safe enough to gather. A person may know, intellectually, that the threat has passed and still breathe as if it has not. The shoulders remain armed. The jaw remains set. Sleep stays shallow. Time never quite steadies. The room is scanned before it is entered. This is why body-based practices are sometimes helpful at the edges of reintegration. Breathwork, walking, yoga, tai chi, qigong, massage, music, art, time in nature, and other grounding practices may help calm the body, restore rhythm, reduce threat, and make it possible to inhabit the body again with less fear. They are not the whole work. They are part of the conditions under which the work becomes possible.

The Five Movements of Reintegration: No single sequence can capture every life. People do not heal in a straight line, and the wounded soul rarely unfolds according to a clean program. Still, certain movements recur with enough regularity to be named. They are not commandments. They are not a treatment protocol. They are the recurring motions by which the fragmented soul begins, slowly and often unevenly, to become a household again.

1. Stabilize the environment. Reintegration cannot occur while the person remains under threat. The soul will not gather while it is still being asked to survive the very conditions that forced it to divide. This is why the environment matters so much. A Reintegration Environment, as I understand it, includes a body that is becoming safer to inhabit, time that is steady enough to be trusted, people who are not themselves sources of danger, work or responsibility that carries meaning rather than chronic humiliation, language honest enough to name what is true, and a future that has not been closed in advance. Safe body, steady time, trustworthy people, meaningful work, honest language, open future, these are not luxuries. They are the architecture within which reintegration becomes thinkable. Without some version of them, the protective system remains on duty for good reason.

2. Recognize the fragments without shame. The second movement is moral in the deepest sense, because shame is one of fragmentation's strongest adhesives. A person must begin to see the inner fragments as survival structures rather than enemies. The frightened part was trying to keep watch. The angry protector was trying to keep power near enough to prevent annihilation. The numb part was trying to spare the system from overload. The appeaser was trying to preserve attachment. The performer was trying to earn safety through excellence or usefulness. The wounded child was carrying what the larger system could not yet bear. The moral witness refused to let the truth disappear. The future-keeping part held some small ember of becoming when everything else narrowed to endurance. None of these should be romanticized, and none of them should rule forever. But they must be recognized with respect before they can loosen their grip. Condemnation drives them further underground. Compassion lets them come into view.

3. Restore communication among the parts. Reintegration is not erasing parts. It is restoring their relationship. The soul must become a household again. In a fragmented life, the parts often function as isolated survival units. One manages work. Another carries terror. Another number. Another pleases. Another keeps the story from being told. Another never sleeps. The person may look unified from the outside while living inside a set of disconnected rooms. The work here is not to force immediate harmony but to reopen communication. What does the protector fear would happen if it stood down? What does the numb part keep from flooding the system? What truth does the wounded part still carry? What does the future-keeping part need in order not to disappear? However, this communication is fostered through reflection, writing, prayer, disciplined attention, careful therapeutic conversation, or other forms of inner honesty the aim is the same: fragments cease to act as strangers and begin to recognize that they belong to one life.

4. Process the wound without overwhelming the soul. At some point, the wound itself must be approached. What happened cannot remain forever sealed in the present tense. Traumatic memory, if reintegration is to deepen, must gradually become past rather than perpetual emergency. But this movement requires caution. The soul cannot be forced into exposure and remain whole. Pacing matters. Safety matters. Bodily regulation matters. Protective parts deserve respect rather than override. Some people undertake this work with trained trauma-informed therapists, and that can be profoundly important. Some approaches may support processing under skilled care, but this chapter is not the place to prescribe methods. The architectural point is simpler: the wound must be met in a way the soul can survive. Not too much. Not too fast. Not with contempt for the defenses that once saved the person's life.

5. Rebuild life as embodied meaning. Reintegration becomes real when life itself begins to change shape. The person rebuilds a coherent story that can hold what happened without being reduced to it. They return to the body not only as a battlefield, but as a place where life can once again be lived. They restore relationships where trust is possible. They participate in the community, however modestly at first. They accept meaningful work or meaningful responsibility. They begin moving again toward becoming. This final movement matters because the soul is not healed in abstraction. Wholeness has to enter time, speech, work, friendship, rest, love, and ordinary practice. Otherwise, reintegration remains an interior idea rather than a lived form.

What these five movements describe, taken together, is not perfection and not the erasure of history. They describe the beginning of wholeness after fracture. The soul does not cease to remember. It learns to remember without being ruled entirely by what happened. It does not become simple. It becomes related. The adaptive structures remain part of life, but they no longer have to govern the whole house alone. And once this becomes visible at the individual level, a larger question immediately presents itself. If persons can fragment and reintegrate, can families, cultures, institutions, and civilizations do the same? That question belongs to the next chapter, because the wounded soul is never only personal. It always lives inside larger structures that can wound, divide, deny, protect, remember, and perhaps, if they become honest enough, begin to heal.

Chapter Twenty-Four
The Civilizational Soul

Collective Shadow and the Possibility of Cultural Individuation

If the soul can fragment at the level of the person, there is no reason in principle to assume that larger human formations are exempt. Families, cultures, institutions, religions, and nations are not persons, and they should not be romanticized as if they possessed a single interior consciousness. But they are organized systems of memory, protection, identity, denial, transmission, and response. They develop recurring patterns. They carry wounds across generations. They defend themselves against what they cannot bear to know. In that limited but important sense, they can become fragmented. A civilization, like a person, can lose communication among its own parts. It can build an official story that excludes too much reality. It can become governed by protective structures that once preserved continuity and later harden into obstacles to truth. The fragmented soul model, applied carefully, gives us a way to think about these collective disorders without collapsing into slogans, partisanship, or fantasy.

Seen in this light, collective fragmentation produces recognizable kinds of parts. A family can have **exile parts**: the member whose pain carries what the family story cannot include, the truth-teller treated as the problem, the addiction, the grief, the abuse, the disability, the shame, the old poverty, the scandal everyone organizes around not naming. A nation can have exiled parts in the form of peoples, histories, regions, languages, or moral facts pushed to the edge of consciousness because they disturb the preferred narrative. Institutions and religions do something similar whenever they bury failure, hide victims, silence dissent, or sacralize forgetfulness. Alongside the exiles come **protector parts**: procedures, orthodoxies, bureaucracies, heroic myths, security structures, moral codes, reputational defenses, and rituals of belonging whose original purpose may have been continuity or survival but whose later function becomes control. Then there are **rage parts**, the collective forms of accumulated humiliation, fear, grievance, and injured identity that are easily mobilized when a system feels threatened. There are **denial parts** that insist nothing happened, nothing is wrong, and nothing needs repair. There are **memory wounds**, the unresolved injuries around which the collective story bends itself generation after generation. And finally, there is **false unity**, the appearance of coherence purchased by suppressing complexity, punishing dissent, and demanding loyalty to a story too thin to hold the truth.

Once these parts are in place, communication within the collective begins to resemble that within a fragmented person. One part of the system speaks in the language of order and necessity. Another carries grief no one wants to hear. Another is permanently vigilant. Another is furious. Another is devoted to preserving appearances. The result is not simply disagreement, which is normal and often healthy, but a breakdown in relational truth. Institutions begin speaking in polished language that no longer corresponds to lived reality. Families repeat founding myths that leave whole rooms of experience in the dark. Religious communities confuse loyalty with silence. Nations speak as though history were a single story of purpose and virtue when, in fact, it contains contradiction, wound, generosity, violence, creation, and denial braided together. A collective in this state can still function, often impressively. It can build, preach, administer, innovate, and defend itself. But it cannot become more whole, because the parts that carry unbearable knowledge are still being treated as enemies of the system rather than bearers of the truth the system needs.

False unity is especially dangerous because it often feels like peace. It can look like social order, institutional discipline, theological certainty, patriotic confidence, or family loyalty. But unity achieved by exiling memory is not wholeness. It is compression. The pressure remains underneath. Memory wounds do not disappear because a culture stops teaching them, because an institution seals its records, because a religion wraps its failures in sacred language, or because a family changes the subject. What is refused at the level of speech often returns at the level of symptom: recurrent outrage, scapegoating, brittle moralism, compulsive repetition of the same conflicts, or the strange inability of a system to respond proportionately to present reality because the past is still acting inside it. This is how intergenerational transmission often works. The later generation may not know the original wound in any detailed way. Yet, it inherits the atmosphere around it: the fear, the silence, the unresolved grievance, the hunger for purity, the suspicion of outsiders, the reflex toward control. A civilization can therefore live inside a wound long after it has forgotten its original name.

What would reintegration mean at this level? Not perfection, not agreement on everything, and not the fantasy of a civilization without conflict. It would mean restoring communication among the collective parts so that memory can re-enter speech, grief can re-enter public life, dissent can serve truth rather than be treated automatically as betrayal, and protective structures can return to their proper place as servants rather than sovereigns. Families do this when they can finally tell the truth about what happened without needing a villain, making the story simple enough. Institutions do it when they can admit failure without collapsing into self-destruction or public theater. Religions do it when confession reaches structure, and not only the private conscience. Nations do it when they develop a narrative capacious enough to hold achievement and wrongdoing in the same account without dissolving into either self-worship or self-hatred. The goal is not the recovery of collective innocence. It is collective maturity: a stronger form of belonging, built on reality rather than repression.

Whether any civilization can sustain that kind of maturity remains an open question. But the alternative is not mysterious. What is not integrated is managed through force, denial, spectacle, or projection, and eventually those instruments fail. The fragmented collective becomes louder, more righteous, more suspicious, and less capable of reality-based self-correction. The lesson is the same here as it was in the individual soul: fragmentation is protective, but it is not final. A people, a church, a university, a family, a nation, each can become organized around exile, protection, rage, denial, wound, and false unity. Each can also, at least in principle, move toward a more difficult honesty. The final chapter must gather what that honesty means. It must ask what kind of humanity becomes possible when the soul is understood not as a relic of the past but as the unfinished architecture through which persons and civilizations alike may yet learn how to become whole enough to carry what transcends them.

Chapter Twenty-Five
The Unfinished Soul

Individuation as Humanity's Deepest Vocation

This book began with a question that is as old as human speech and as immediate as private suffering: what is the soul, if the old words are not dead and the new words are not enough? By the time one has traveled through Egypt, Greece, Jerusalem, Hippo, Andalusia, Toledo, Zurich, the clinic, the wounded body, the fractured family, the algorithmic feed, and the civilizational crisis of our own hour, the question has not become smaller. It has become more inhabited. The soul has shown itself not as a superstition waiting to be outgrown, nor as a sentimental residue left behind by modern intelligence, but as a recurring discovery about what a human being actually is. The traditions disagreed, as serious traditions do. They named different dimensions, emphasized different powers, and argued over origins and ends. Yet beneath the differences, a shape emerged with remarkable consistency. The soul is the dimension of the human being in which life becomes more than reaction, more than mechanism, more than role. It is the organizing depth in which memory, conscience, desire, suffering, relation, imagination, and transcendence meet.

The full arc matters. The soul began, in some of our oldest records, as cosmic breath not private property but participation in a living order. In Egypt and the Hebrew world alike, breath meant more than respiration. It meant animation by what exceeds the person, life received rather than self-generated, a structure of belonging between the human and the more-than-human. It then became moral conscience, not in the thin sense of rule-following but in the deeper sense that the soul is answerable, weighable, responsive to truth. The heart could be judged. The self could be called. Then, in Greece and the medieval synthesis that followed, the soul became rational substance and substantial form: the principle of life, intelligibility, and inner order, capable of thought, virtue, and orientation toward truth. Much was gained in that refinement. But something was also narrowed. Under modernity, the soul gradually collapsed into mind, and mind into consciousness, and consciousness into the self-report of the thinking ego. The old depth was not argued away so much as reduced to what the rational subject could certify about itself. This is one of the great diminutions in the history of human self-understanding.

What modern trauma study, depth psychology, and lived experience have forced back into view is that the soul cannot be understood if we look only at the uninjured self. The modern person did not merely lose the concept of the soul in philosophy. The modern person also suffered in ways that exposed the inadequacy of the older models when they were taken as complete—trauma revealed fracture. Dissociation revealed multiplicity. The traumatized psyche did not behave like a unified, rational substance because, under conditions of overwhelm, it was trying to survive rather than satisfy metaphysics. But the fracture, rightly understood, did not disprove the soul. It disclosed another dimension of it. The soul reappeared not as a ghost, not as a doctrine, and not merely as a mood, but as adaptive architecture. It turned out to be dynamic rather than static, structural rather than sentimental, capable of changing form without losing essence. It did not fragment because it was weak. It fragmented because it was protecting the person at all costs. That recognition changes the moral atmosphere of the entire discussion. Fragmentation is not a shameful failure. It is intelligent survival. Reintegration is not the correction of a defect. It is the completion of a protective process that was never meant to be final.

That is why the later chapters of this book had to be moved where they were. Once the soul is seen as layered, with a Core Self, a Narrative Self, an Adaptive Self, and the possibility of an Integrated Self, the task becomes clearer. The work is not to simplify the person into some fantasy of purity. It is to restore communication where trauma, shame, fear, and history forced isolation. Reintegration begins in environment, attention, relationship, narrative, and agency because the soul gathers under conditions rather than abstractions, and because becoming depends on those conditions being rebuilt in lived form. And once this is visible in the individual, it becomes impossible not to see its larger implications. Families can fragment. Institutions can fragment. Religions can fragment. Nations can fragment. Civilizations can exile their own truth, organize themselves around protective structures, rehearse rage, deny memory, and mistake false unity for peace. A post-fracture humanity, if such a thing is possible, would be humanity on the far side of that recognition: no longer naive about fracture, no longer ashamed of adaptation, and no longer willing to build personal or collective identity on denial. It would be understood that wholeness is not innocence recovered. The relation is restored.

This brings us to the final correction the book has been moving toward all along. Wholeness must come before transcendence, or at least close enough beside it that transcendence does not become one more way of leaving the wounded life behind. The soul is not completed by going upward alone. It is completed when what has been touched above can be carried back through the wounded layers and into speech, work, friendship, conscience, embodiment, and history. True transcendence does not cancel the human. It deepens it. It does not excuse the wound. It returns through the wound as wisdom. This is why reintegration matters so much. It is not a therapeutic side-concern added late to an otherwise philosophical book. It is the condition under which the soul can carry its own depth without splitting under it, and the condition under which any culture can remain human while trying to become more than its current violences, denials, and simplifications. The soul, as this book has tried to show, is non-mortal not because the ego floats away untouched, but because the soul's deeper architecture persists through change, through fracture, through history, through re-formation, still oriented toward wholeness.

So the final word is not mastery. It is becoming. The soul began as breath in the cosmos, became conscience before truth, became substantial form and rational principle, was narrowed into mind, was fractured under the force of trauma and history, reappeared as adaptive architecture, and now stands before us again as the unfinished form of a post-fracture humanity. That phrase means nothing grand unless it means something intimate: a humanity capable of surviving without worshiping survival, capable of remembering without being ruled only by memory, capable of integrating its fragments without pretending they never saved it, capable of carrying transcendence back into ordinary life without inflation or escape. We are not finished, creatures. That is our danger, and it is also our hope. The soul's journey has not ended because the soul's work is not to arrive at a sterile completion. It is to become whole enough to live truthfully, deeply, and with enough embodied courage that what is highest in us does not float free of what is most wounded. If that happens, even imperfectly, then the old word "soul" will not merely have been recovered. It will have become usable again for the age now arriving.

All references follow Chicago/Turabian style, with entries arranged alphabetically by author's surname.

Aquinas, Thomas. *Summa Theologiae*. Translated by the Fathers of the English Dominican Province. New York: Benziger Brothers, 1948.

Aristotle. *De Anima*. Translated by Christopher Shields. Oxford: Clarendon Press, 2016.

Assmann, Jan. *Death and Salvation in Ancient Egypt*. Translated by David Lorton. Ithaca: Cornell University Press, 2005.

Assmann, Jan. *The Mind of Egypt: History and Meaning in the Time of the Pharaohs*. Translated by Andrew Jenkins. New York: Metropolitan Books, 2002.

Augustine of Hippo. *Confessions*. Translated by Henry Chadwick. Oxford: Oxford University Press, 1991.

Chadwick, Henry. *Augustine of Hippo: A Life*. Oxford: Oxford University Press, 2009.

Conforti, Michael. *Field, Form, and Fate: Patterns in Mind, Nature, and Experience*. New Orleans: Spring Journal Books, 2003.

Corbin, Henry. *Creative Imagination in the Sufism of Ibn 'Arabi*. Translated by Ralph Manheim. Princeton: Princeton University Press, 1969.

Corbin, Henry. *Alone with the Alone: Creative Imagination in the Sufism of Ibn 'Arabi*. Princeton: Princeton University Press, 1997.

Cottingham, John. *Descartes*. Oxford: Blackwell, 1986.

Crawford, Kate. *Atlas of AI: Power, Politics, and the Planetary Costs of Artificial Intelligence*. New Haven: Yale University Press, 2021.

Davies, Brian. *The Thought of Thomas Aquinas*. Oxford: Clarendon Press, 1992.

Descartes, René. *Meditations on First Philosophy*. Translated by John Cottingham. Cambridge: Cambridge University Press, 1986.

Edinger, Edward F. *Anatomy of the Psyche: Alchemical Symbolism in Psychotherapy*. La Salle, IL: Open Court, 1985.

Eliade, Mircea. *Shamanism: Archaic Techniques of Ecstasy*. Translated by Willard Trask. Princeton: Princeton University Press, 1964.

Freud, Sigmund. *The Interpretation of Dreams*. In *The Standard Edition of the Complete Psychological Works of Sigmund Freud*, vols. 4–5. Translated by James Strachey. London: Hogarth Press, 1953.

Freud, Sigmund. *Civilization and Its Discontents*. In *The Standard Edition*, vol. 21. Translated by James Strachey. London: Hogarth Press, 1961.

Herman, Judith L. *Trauma and Recovery: The Aftermath of Violence—from Domestic Abuse to Political Terror*. New York: Basic Books, 1992.

Hillman, James. *Re-Visioning Psychology*. New York: Harper & Row, 1975.

Hollis, James. *The Middle Passage: From Misery to Meaning in Midlife*. Toronto: Inner City Books, 1993.

Hornung, Erik. *Conceptions of God in Ancient Egypt: The One and the Many*. Translated by John Baines. Ithaca: Cornell University Press, 1982.

Hornung, Erik. *The Ancient Egyptian Books of the Afterlife*. Translated by David Lorton. Ithaca: Cornell University Press, 1999.

Hume, David. *A Treatise of Human Nature*. Edited by L. A. Selby-Bigge; revised by P. H. Nidditch. Oxford: Clarendon Press, 1978.

Ibn Arabi, Muhyiddin. *The Bezels of Wisdom (Fusus al-Hikam)*. Translated by R. W. J. Austin. New York: Paulist Press, 1980.

Ibn Sina (Avicenna). *The Book of Salvation (Kitab al-Najat)*. Edited and translated by Fazlur Rahman. London: Oxford University Press, 1952.

John of the Cross. *The Collected Works of St. John of the Cross*. Translated by Kieran Kavanaugh and Otilio Rodriguez. Washington, DC: ICS Publications, 1991.

Jung, C. G. *Collected Works of C. G. Jung*. Edited by Herbert Read, Michael Fordham, and Gerhard Adler. 20 vols. Princeton: Princeton University Press, 1953–1979.

Jung, C. G. *The Red Book: Liber Novus*. Edited by Sonu Shamdasani. Translated by Mark Kyburz, John Peck, and Sonu Shamdasani. New

York: W. W. Norton, 2009.

Jung, C. G. *Memories, Dreams, Reflections*. Edited by Aniela Jaffé. Translated by Richard and Clara Winston. New York: Pantheon Books, 1962.

Kaufmann, Walter. *Nietzsche: Philosopher, Psychologist, Antichrist*. 4th ed. Princeton: Princeton University Press, 1974.

Kimbles, Samuel L. *Phantom Narratives: The Unseen Contributions of Culture to Psyche*. Lanham, MD: Rowman & Littlefield, 2014.

Locke, John. *An Essay Concerning Human Understanding*. Edited by P. H. Nidditch. Oxford: Clarendon Press, 1975.

Matthew, Iain. *The Impact of God: Soundings from St. John of the Cross*. London: Hodder & Stoughton, 1995.

Moore, Thomas. *Care of the Soul: A Guide for Cultivating Depth and Sacredness in Everyday Life*. New York: HarperCollins, 1992.

Myers, Frederic W. H. *Human Personality and Its Survival of Bodily Death*. 2 vols. London: Longmans, Green, 1903.

Nasr, Seyyed Hossein. *Three Muslim Sages: Avicenna, Suhrawardi, Ibn 'Arabi*. Cambridge, MA: Harvard University Press, 1964.

Nietzsche, Friedrich. *Thus Spoke Zarathustra*. Translated by Walter Kaufmann. New Viking, 1966.

Nietzsche, Friedrich. *The Gay Science*. Translated by Walter Kaufmann. New York: Vintage, 1974.

O'Donnell, James J. *Augustine: Sinner and Saint*. London: Profile Books, 2005.

O'Meara, Dominic J. *Plotinus: An Introduction to the Enneads*. Oxford: Clarendon Press, 1993.

Pedersen, Johannes. *Israel: Its Life and Culture*. 4 vols. London: Oxford University Press, 1926–1940.

Plato. *Complete Works*. Edited by John M. Cooper. Indianapolis: Hackett, 1997.

Plotinus. *The Enneads*. Translated by Stephen MacKenna; abridged by John Dillon. London: Penguin, 1991.

Rist, John M. *Stoic Philosophy*. Cambridge: Cambridge University

Press, 1969.

Schwartz, Richard C. *No Bad Parts: Healing Trauma and Restoring Wholeness with the Internal Family Systems Model*. Boulder, CO: Sounds True, 2021.

Singer, Thomas, and Samuel L. Kimbles, eds. *The Cultural Complex: Contemporary Jungian Perspectives on Psyche and Society*. Hove: Brunner-Routledge, 2004.

Stump, Eleonore. *Aquinas*. London: Routledge, 2003.

van der Kolk, Bessel. *The Body Keeps the Score: Brain, Mind, and Body in the Healing of Trauma*. New York: Viking, 2014.

Wolff, Hans Walter. *Anthropology of the Old Testament*. Translated by Margaret Kohl. Philadelphia: Fortress Press, 1974.

Zuboff, Shoshana. *The Age of Surveillance Capitalism: The Fight for a Human Future at the New Frontier of Power*. New York: PublicAffairs, 2019.

About the Author

Albert Baye Schriber, PhD, did not come to the study of the soul through abstraction but through necessity. Long before he became a systems analyst, philosopher, and developmental theorist, he was a boy trying to make sense of fragmentation, his own and that of the people he loved. The early wounds that shaped his inner life became the ground from which his lifelong question emerged: *What happens to a soul under pressure, and how does it find its way back to coherence?*

His path was not linear. He served as a Navy electronics technician, learning the discipline of systems thinking before he had language for the systems inside himself. He spent nearly three decades at Hewlett-Packard as a computer specialist and program manager, mastering the architectures of complex machines while quietly studying the architectures of inner life. Along the way, he earned a PhD in philosophy, drawn to the thinkers who wrestled with the same questions that had shaped him since childhood.

Schriber writes not as a clinician but as a man who has lived the realities he describes. Years of therapy, spiritual inquiry, and philosophical study converged into a single conviction: the soul is not fragile. It is adaptive, intelligent, and capable of reintegration even after profound division. His work blends metaphysics, developmental psychology, trauma theory, and systems analysis into a unified framework he calls the Layered Soul.

He is the author of metaphysical nonfiction and literary fiction, and his research is deeply informed by his role as a grandfather, witnessing, with both love and alarm, how algorithmic environments shape the inner lives of today's youth. His writing is dedicated to the wounded who seek hope, to the healers who guide them, and to anyone who has ever felt the quiet ache of a divided inner world.

Albert lives in Peachtree City, Georgia, where he continues to write, teach, and explore the evolving architecture of the human soul.

www.ingramcontent.com/pod-product-compliance
Lightning Source LLC
LaVergne TN
LVHW090418210926
848480LV00002B/615

* 9 7 9 8 9 5 0 8 4 2 0 1 6 *